Everything in Christ

DONALD ENGLISH, General Secretary of the Methodist Church Division of Home Mission, is a distinguished scholar and preacher; Past President of the Methodist Conference and member of the World Methodist Council, he has taught New Testament studies in Britain and Africa, been a circuit minister, and written extensively.

DAVID BUCKTROUT, formerly a teacher of Art and Design, is a Methodist minister who explores the links between the Arts and Christian faith; responding to requests from churches, he runs 'worship workshops', where ordinary people are encouraged to express the Faith in artistic ways. Workshop members have contributed poetry and prayers to this book; the illustrations are of ordinary folk, the people one might meet in a worship workshop.

● The Bible Reading Fellowship was founded 'to encourage the systematic and intelligent reading of the Bible, to emphasize its spiritual message and to take advantage of new light shed on Holy Scripture'.

● Over the years the Fellowship has proved a trustworthy guide for those who want an open, informed and contemporary approach to the Bible. It retains a sense of the unique authority of Scripture as a prime means by which God communicates.

● As an ecumenical organization, the Fellowship embraces all Christian traditions and its readers are to be found in most parts of the world.

Everything in Christ

DONALD ENGLISH

with illustrations by
David Bucktrout

The Bible Reading Fellowship
Warwick House
25 Buckingham Palace Road
London SW1W 0PP

First published 1988
© BRF 1988

Acknowledgements

Bible quotations are for the most part taken from the New International Version, © 1973, 1979, 1984 by the International Bible Society.

Cover design: David Bucktrout
Printed by Bocardo Press Ltd, Oxford

PREFACE

Personal preferences for Lenten reading vary greatly. We are not likely to go wrong, however, if we engage in serious study of some part of the Bible, seeking to apply it to ourselves and to life around us. Many great turning points in the life of the church have originated from such modest beginnings.

In 1988, Methodists all round the world celebrate the dramatic conversion experiences of John and Charles Wesley, 250 years ago. Whatever those experiences involved, they were the turning point for the missionary effectiveness of the Wesleys. Methodism grew on this foundation. At heart it involved proclamation of the biblical message, and response to that message in every part of human life. Now, 250 years later, we are attempting a similar task in a very different context.

The task is not a simple one. It involves the reader in a sympathetic attempt to understand the setting in which the passages were written, the words used to express the meaning, the principles which emerge, and how they relate to our lives today.

It is not easy, but it is extremely rewarding. The Bible is the basic literature of Christianity. Its pages contain the story of God's preparation for the coming of Jesus Christ, the events of that short and stormy ministry, the claims that are made about Jesus and the way of believing and living which resulted.

In the New Testament letters we see attempts to address particular situations in the light of the Christian message. The Colossian letter is written to deal with a type of false teaching which drew out from Paul some profound exposition of the gospel and what it means to believe in it.

We could scarcely find a better way to take our journey through Lent than in company with the great apostle as he defends, explains and applies faith in Jesus Christ.

D. E.

What is a Worship Workshop?

A Worship Workshop is an opportunity for people of all ages to use the Arts to explore aspects of the Christian Faith.

Often taking place on a Saturday, a workshop invites everyone who will join in to paint, model, write, sing, dance, etc., in order to express thoughts about life and Christianity. Though an end in itself, the workshop often leads on to Sunday worship where many of the ideas explored on the Saturday can be developed in Family Worship.

Workshops allow us all to see that our God thoughts are important, and that we can make a contribution to the worship of our church. Workshops can help us see things in new ways. They are an opportunity for inviting people into the life of the local church.

David Bucktrout

CONTENTS

THE <u>POSITION</u> OF <u>COLOSSAE</u>

DAILY READINGS

Ash Wednesday   Colossians 1:1–2

Paul, an apostle of Christ Jesus by the will of God, and Timothy our brother,
To the holy and faithful brothers in Christ at Colosse:
Grace and peace to you from God our Father.

Colossae

Where we live is an extremely important part of our lives. It sets the stage for most of the things we do, and it is responsible for many of the influences upon us. Village, town and city life are not the same thing. Living in an African family compound is not like living in a British surburban semi. The history, tradition, culture, life-style and values all influence us constantly. Lebanon, Liverpool and Lucerne are not just miles apart; they are worlds apart. What is more, they provide different contexts for the Christians who live their lives there.

Paul's readers lived at Colossae, a city in the Lycus valley, 100 miles or so east of Ephesus. A main trade route from Ephesus to the Eastern world ran right through Colossae. Wool and weaving were its two main commercial products and Colossae was once a very important city. By the time Paul wrote this letter, however, it was considerably overshadowed by two other cities, Laodicea and Hierapolis. As one commentator put it, Colossae was probably the least important city to which Paul addressed a letter. It was still a highly developed cultural centre, however, with variety of races represented. There seems also to have been a mixture of Jews and Gentiles in the church at Colossae, with the Gentiles predominant. Epaphras, the evangelist, is referred to as 'one of you' (4:12) and he was a Gentile. In 1:21 the word 'aliens' is used, and the parallel from Ephesians 2:12 suggests it means aliens from the commonwealth of Israel. In 1:27 Paul affirms 'how great among the Gentiles are the riches of the glory of this mystery, which is Christ in you, the hope of glory'. There are no more than five Old Testament allusions in the whole letter, suggesting that he did not expect the readers to know the Old Testament well.

Overall, therefore, the Christians were in a context where the past was brighter than the present or the future, where something which gave a sense of superiority over others might well be welcomed, and where the likelihood of some religious concoction from various faiths was high. As we shall see, that is precisely what happened at Colossae.

We do well, therefore, today, to consider how our context influences us. We must also ask how the gospel message addresses our situation. As the biblical people would have put it, 'What is the word of the Lord for today?', locally, nationally and at the world level.

It need not all be judgement upon us. We do have much to answer for, in the continued existence of so many poor and refugees, in the use of enormous resources for weapons of war, in the ridiculous importance we attach to material possessions and outward appearance. But there are positive things too — medical advances, communications techniques in disaster situations, a growing sense that every human being deserves a certain quality of life.

The question is how the Christian good news interacts with all that is happening. In the Swiss Alps I stood on a peak at Manlichen, looking down with binoculars at the two villages of Wengen and Lauterbrunnen, lying side by side far below. When, however, a few days later I visited Lauterbrunnen, I discovered that the two villages were not side by side at all, but that Wengen was considerably higher than Lauterbrunnen. But it took a change of perspective to see it. Paul wrote to Colossae to show how the Christian gospel related to their setting. It is the privilege of the Christian to do the same in every generation and place.

Prayer   Help me, Lord, to be properly aware of the contexts in which I live my life. May I be sensitive to the pressures exerted upon me and upon those around me, from the prevailing culture. Enable me to see where the gospel of Jesus Christ affirms the assumptions, attitudes and actions of contemporary life, and where it passes judgement on them. Then let me live according to that gospel, so that values higher than those of my culture may be clear to all.

Thursday after Ash Wednesday   Colossians 1:1–2 (page 9)

Paul

Every Christian knows about Paul. He towers like a Colossus across the pages of the New Testament. Apart from the Gospels and Acts he dominates the teaching documents of Christianity. Through Paul, Augustine's life was changed. Through Paul, Martin Luther grasped the great doctrine of salvation by grace through faith. Through Paul, Jean Calvin came to his convictions about

God's sovereignty. Through Paul, John Wesley's heart was strangely warmed. Through Paul, Karl Barth challenged the whole theological world of his time. No Christian will ever hold the position Paul held. Few will achieve the heights of those quoted above, whose own lives were transformed through his writing. Yet that does not put Paul beyond our reach, or out of our class.

Paul is an example of how God doesn't waste anything! Christians in the earliest days were learning to fear him beyond any others. He was so well grounded in the Hebrew scriptures and traditions that no one would choose to take him on in a public debate. His level of practice of the Hebrew faith was exemplary. His upbringing had been all that a young Jew could require. He had then received the best intellectual training available. And he was zealous! When others believed the Christians to be wrong, and said so; Paul both said so and did something about it. He sets out all these qualifications in Philippians 3:4–6. What the Christians could not know, and what Paul did not know, was that all those qualities and all that expertise were to be used to God's own glory in the service of Christ. It was because Paul already had such a background and ability that God would use him as the prime exponent of the Christian faith, once he was into it.

There is much extravagant language amongst Christians about being 'an entirely different person' after conversion. It is customary to do everything possible in testimonies to denigrate the pre-conversion days in order to elevate the post-conversion days. And, of course, there is a deep truth here. In Christ, as

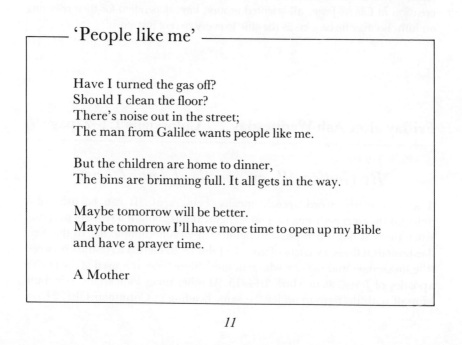

'People like me'

Have I turned the gas off?
Should I clean the floor?
There's noise out in the street;
The man from Galilee wants people like me.

But the children are home to dinner,
The bins are brimming full. It all gets in the way.

Maybe tomorrow will be better.
Maybe tomorrow I'll have more time to open up my Bible
and have a prayer time.

A Mother

Paul taught the Corinthians, there is 'a new creation' (2 Corinthians 5:17). But many of the building materials for the new creation are carried over from the old creation! What is new is their re-orientation around Christ, submitting to him and finding meaning and power in him. But God transforms and uses much that we were, in making us what he wishes us to be.

Paul is also in our league for another reason. He is an example of the fact that you cannot know all that God is doing simply by observing Christians. In one sense Paul's conversion on the road to Damascus had nothing to do with the Christians at all (Acts 9:1–9). There was not a single Christian in sight when the risen Christ confronted him. It is a very salutary reminder that the advance of the kingdom of God does not depend primarily on the efforts of Christians, but on the grace of God. No doubt God used the wonderful witness of Stephen, that first martyr, whose death Paul witnessed (Acts 7:58). More certainly God used Ananias to guide Paul about his place in the Christian family and about God's purpose for his future ministry (Acts 9:10–19). But it is God's grace that lies at the heart of our faith, and we can be grateful for that.

We may reflect today on how much our faith depends on God's grace and not our efforts.

Prayer Thank you, Father, for giants in the faith like the apostle Paul. Thank you, too, that he has much in common with us. Help me to a greater awareness of the gifts you have given me, the experiences you have afforded me, and the lessons you have taught me. May they all be gathered into my life as a new creation in Christ Jesus, all oriented around him, dependent for their meaning on him. So may he be seen as the clue to every part of my life.

Friday after Ash Wednesday   **Colossians 1:1–2 (page 9)**

'By God's will, an apostle of Jesus Christ'

The root of the word apostle means 'being sent'. It can be used of a delegation, an expedition, or a messenger. It has about it a sense of purpose, since there is not much point in being sent with nothing to do! In the New Testament it finds a variety of uses. In John 13:16 there is a contrast between 'the messenger and the one who sent him'. Sometimes it is used of the twelve apostles of Jesus, as in Mark 3:14–15. At other times Paul seems to include himself with that group under the same heading (1 Corinthians 9:1, 2 Cor-

inthians 12:12; Galatians 2:7–8). Again it can be used of a wider group still, including people like Barnabas (Acts 14:14), and others (Romans 16:7).

Paul's own claim to apostleship, which he argued strongly because it was denied by some, is based on a specific foundation. He has seen the risen Christ (1 Corinthians 9:1). He has had a divine call (Galatians 1:1). He performs the signs of an apostle in his ministry (2 Corinthians 12:12). He also feels that God prepared him long ago for apostleship (Galatians 1:15, cp. Jeremiah 1:5).

There is much debate in the contemporary church about apostleship. The argument is used in relation to ordained ministry, or episcopacy, or papacy. It is also used in the house church movements in connection with structures of leadership there. The fact that in the first century it could be used both so specifically (about Paul, for example), and so generally (about a large number of others), should warn us against understanding it so much in terms of structures, or status, or personalized claims. We do far better to note the marks of apostleship as belonging to the early church, and demonstrated particularly in the lives of some who had various leadership responsibilities. For the present we need to ask the most general question of whether our churches bear the marks of apostleship: obedience to God's call, awareness of the presence of the risen Christ, doing apostolic work. Within the context of the answer we may wish to observe that certain people demonstrate those characteristics in their ministry and life, but that is a secondary matter to the prime question for the whole church. To assume that certain people, because they hold certain office, are automatically 'apostolic' is to put the cart before the horse.

We can gather these matters together in terms of the life of our own church. In what ways has God been preparing it for its apostolic tasks? How is the call of God perceived by us, corporately and individually, and how are we to be obedient to it? In what ways are we made aware of the presence of the risen Christ in our personal lives and in our corporate fellowship, worship and service? What are the apostolic tasks we ought to be performing in our world today, and in the particular setting of our own church?

One last reflection on apostleship has to do with direction. 'Being sent' is about receiving a command at the centre, the effect of which is to move us from that point towards the circumference. We may conclude that 'apostolic signs' will always contain pressure to move out beyond the context where the call was received, into the area where the call has not yet been received or obeyed. Apostleship and mission are extremely close companions.

Prayer Lord, I hesitate to call myself an apostle but I'm glad to belong to an apostolic church. Please help all your people to show the signs of apostleship: obedience to your call, awareness to the presence of Christ, involvement in the work to which you send them. So may others look at the face of the church and see the eyes of Christ looking out at them.

Saturday after Ash Wednesday   Colossians 1:1–2 (page 9)

'And from our brother Timothy'

Thoughts on apostleship ('being sent') lead naturally to Timothy, because almost every time Paul mentions him, he is sending Timothy somewhere! In

1 Thessalonians 3:2 'we sent Timothy'. In 1 Corinthians 4:17 'I sent to you Timothy'. In Philippians 2:19 'I hope to send Timothy'. Whatever else he knew, Timothy understood what it meant to be a 'sent man'.

He was probably with Paul in prison for some time, ministering to the apostle and helping him with his work. I have in my study a print of Rembrandt's painting, 'The Apostle Paul in Prison'. It is one of the few paintings that move me to tears. The old man is sitting on his bed, surrounded by the books and parchments that were so vital to his continuing ministry from prison. The sword stands there, too. The old man has one foot out of a sandal, the other in. His left hand, with veins very prominent, holds a pen; the right hand is up to the chin. The hair is straggly and back off the forehead. The eyes are deep brown; reflective of strength, pain and hope; and they stare out into the distance. How lonely and how confined for the travelling preacher! But there was Timothy. Paul says of him in Philippians 2:20, 'I have no one else like him'. And later, 'Timothy has proved himself, because as a son with his father he has served with me in the work of the gospel' (Philippians 2:22). Timothy can be trusted, relied upon.

I welcome the modern openness developing among Christians. I am glad that in groups and one-to-one relationships people are able to admit their needs and are able to receive counsel and ministry. At the same time I am nervous about the result where people seem to depend on being counselled, and where more and more Christians need someone to counsel. We are in danger of developing the spiritual equivalent of the 'You don't look well today' syndrome. Christianity is certainly about trusting God and benefitting from fellowship. It is equally certainly *not* about having to lean on others all the time. A friend of mine used to warn young Christians against being 'filleted Christians, with no backbone'. Paul thanks his Philippian readers in Philippians 4:13f that they shared his troubles; but he is also able to claim humbly, 'I can do everything through him who gives me strength.'

Midst all the emphasis on gifts today, and on signs and wonders — an emphasis which has filled a gap in our Christian experience — there remains an even greater need, for strong, reliable Christians who can be counted on to stand firm in the most difficult days. Timothy was one such.

Of course strong Christians don't just happen. Timothy had had enormous privilege spiritually. In 2 Timothy 1:5 we read of his faithful grandmother Lois and mother Eunice. (Why no mention of the men in the family? Were these women believers in spite of their husbands' unbelief?) The same faith they passed on to Timothy, on whom Paul too had laid hands for the giving of a gift from God. It is surely no surprise that in this setting Paul goes on to affirm that 'God did not give us a spirit of timidity, but a spirit of power, of love and of self-discipline' (2 Timothy 2:7). No wonder Timothy can be trusted. He has been raised for it. Not all can have the privilege of a

Christian home: but all can receive God's gifts of power, love and self-discipline.

We need to grow such Christians in the church today, and we can begin by asking God to make us like that.

Prayer I am grateful, O God, that you did not give your people a spirit of timidity, but a spirit of power, of love and of self-discipline. Grant that I may know that power daily at work in my life; that your love may be the energy which influences everything I think, say and do; and that my self-discipline may set me free for your service.

Questions for consideration by individuals or groups

1. How does our culture and context influence our way of being Christians? How ought our faith to affect our culture and context?

2. What would you say were the signs of an apostolic church? How could your church show those signs more clearly?

'Saints and faithful brethren'

Paul turns now to the people who will read this letter. He calls them 'saints'; one of the most misunderstood words in the Christian vocabulary. We know it best as a description of outstanding Christians, set apart as such by sections of the Christian church. But this is not its meaning in the New Testament.

Writers like Paul use the word 'saint' to describe all believers in Jesus Christ. It does not apply only to those who have achieved a certain level of sanctity. For example, Paul's letters to the church at Corinth show how far many of the Christians there had fallen from Christian standards. Yet he still begins his first letter to them by addressing them as 'saints'. They were anything but saints according to the more popular view!

Paul could address them as saints because the word primarily describes their *status*, rather than their *condition*. Coming from a root meaning 'cutting' and then 'separated' (since when you cut a piece of cloth you separate one part from the other), it had come to mean 'set apart' or 'dedicated'. By reason of their faith in Jesus, signified in their baptism, these people were counted as 'set apart', or 'dedicated' to God. That is the status, the standing, of every Christian; however good or bad a Christian he or she is. In Christ we are set apart for God — saints. Even the Corinthian Christians, with all their faults, had that status.

Of course the Christians in the first century were told that they were saints in order that they might live like saints. This is why Paul, at the beginning of his first letter to the Corinthians says they are 'saints who are called to be holy', but the word 'saints' and the word 'holy' are from the same root. It could be translated to mean that they are 'saints who are called to be saints'! The first use of the word describes their *standing*. They are 'in Christ', 'set apart'. The second describes the *condition*. They are to seek to live as people who are in Christ. Their holy life is meant to reflect their holy status. What God has done for us *'in Christ'* is a challenge to us to become *'like Christ'*. Both meanings are incorporated in Paul's use of the word to the Colossians at the outset of his letter to them.

But the Colossians are also addressed as 'faithful brothers' (Paul would have written 'brothers and sisters' if he had been sending his letter today). Their position as Christians cannot be understood only in terms of their relationship to God in Christ. It is also about their relationship to one another as brothers and sisters. To belong to God in Christ means to belong to God's family in Christ. In his letter to the Romans Paul describes his church under the image of a body.

There is a very deep mystery here, but its implication is clear. I belong to every other Christian, and every other Christian belongs to me. Those with whom I disagree most strongly are mine, and I am theirs, not because we chose or accepted one another for reasons of personality, theology or practice, but because God in Christ has chosen and accepted us. We do not have to agree with other Christians about their theology or practice, but we do have to affirm one another as brother and sister Christians. After that the discussion about truth and practice can begin but within the acknowledged membership of the family of God.

When Igor Stravinsky's 'Rite of Spring' was first performed, audiences disliked it. They thought it too vigorous and boisterous, ignoring musical conventions of the day. Stravinsky's reply was that in Russia you can hear Spring bursting out. (Having heard ice cracking in the Swiss Alps, I can believe it.) Whatever the audiences preferred, the facts were against them. However attached we are to our denominational differences, the facts are against us. We Christians belong to one another inextricably.

Prayer Lord, I find it hard to think of myself as a saint. I need help to understand more deeply what it means to be 'set apart' for you in daily life, and then to put it into practice. Thank you that you see me as a saint. Please help me to live up to your expectations of me. I'm grateful not to be doing all this on my own. It's hard to picture what it means to belong to every other Christian, and to have every other Christian belonging to me. We're quite a family! Enable me to welcome them into my life more.

Lent 1/Monday   **Colossians 1:1–2 (page 9)**

'Grace and peace'

Paul now combines a Greek and a Hebrew greeting in order to show the enormous privilege of the Christian.

Grace is God's love in action. It cannot be earned or deserved. It flows out of the heart of God's own being. It is more easily illustrated than defined.

In Matthew 20:1–16 there is a story told by Jesus of the vineyard owner who set labourers to work at different points throughout the day, but paid them all the same wage at the end. Even reading the story now, so long after it was told, one feels within oneself the outrage of the men who had worked all day and then received the same pay as men who had worked only one hour.

When these men made their complaint, however, the owner pointed out that he had paid them the wage they had agreed. Concerning what he had paid the others, he asks, 'Don't I have the right to do as I wish with my own money, or are you jealous because I am generous?' (Matthew 20:15 Good News Bible).

This is the heart of grace. It deals with each of us according to our need and not according to our deserving. The men who worked the whole shift felt they deserved what they got. The rest were grateful *not* to be treated according to what they had earned!

As a parable of the kingdom, this story of Jesus is a reminder to us all that when we place our lives under the scrutiny of a holy, loving God, all talk of getting what we deserve becomes redundant. We have no claim on him except that we need what we don't deserve — his warm acceptance of us so that we may experience his love in our lives. This he gives us by grace, supremely shown in the life, death, resurrection and ascension of Jesus on our behalf.

This is why the Reformers struggled so hard to proclaim that salvation is 'by grace through faith'. We don't earn it; God gives it. We don't create it; we receive it. God's graciousness is a cornerstone of the gospel message. Paul can greet the Colossian Christians as saints because God is gracious.

The other half of the greeting is 'peace'. This is based on the lovely Hebrew word *'shalom'* which we often hear in songs today. Shalom is not peace simply in the sense of absence of war, though it includes that. Shalom is a deep inward assurance that all is well because God is ultimately in control. It is Jesus sleeping in the prow of a storm-tossed boat. It is the risen Christ greeting his disciples in the midst of their turmoil and despair after his death. It is the conviction that there is a way for the world's wrongs to be righted, and that justice will prevail in God's kingdom.

It is not therefore simply a passive sense that we can 'leave it all to God'. Peace carries with it the impetus to work in harmony with God's controlling presence, to respond without anxiety to difficult situations, to look beyond immediately hurtful experiences to the eventual purpose involved, and to give oneself to working against the injustice in the world which so denies the presence of God's shalom.

There is theological sense in the order of this greeting. It is God's grace which makes it possible for us to enter into his peace.

Prayer Father God, I don't understand why you are so gracious, but I'm glad you are. Your generosity is clear in the variety of nature, colour, size, species, ability, seasons, night and day. Forgive us our lack of graciousness to one another. However could we think it right to use nuclear fission in order to blow one another up, or chemical research to produce nerve gas, while half the world has less food than it needs, and drastically inadequate medical care? Help us to follow the path of grace — yours to us and ours to one another — in search of the goal of peace which is also your gift.

Lent 1/Tuesday   Colossians 1:3–8

We always thank God, the Father of our Lord Jesus Christ, when we pray for you, because we have heard of your faith in Christ Jesus and of the love you have for all the saints — the faith and love that spring from the hope that is stored up for you in heaven and that you have already heard about in the word of truth, the gospel that has come to you. All over the world this gospel is bearing fruit and growing, just as it has been doing among you since the day you heard it and understood God's grace in all its truth. You learned it from Epaphras, our dear fellow-servant, who is a faithful minister of Christ on our behalf, and who also told us of your love in the Spirit.

'We always give thanks'

It is clear that Paul had never been to Colossae. He hears about the Colossian Christianity through Epaphras (vv.4 and 8). He was now in prison with even less likelihood of getting to see them but, as Archdeacon Herbert Cragg once said, 'Colossae could still be reached by way of the throne of grace'. Prayer crosses all boundaries. Paul neither defends nor explains why he prays for them. It is so fundamental for the Christian to turn to God, the Father of our Lord Jesus Christ, that explanation is not necessary. It would be like explaining breathing. You only need the explanation when you are ill.

'We always thank God' has been taken by some to mean that we should thank God *for* everything. I understand the intention of such teaching. It helps us to affirm that God can bring good out of the worst things in life. We know that is true because out of the worst event in human history, the crucifying of the Son of God, the good news of the gospel was created. Yet to thank God *for* everything also masks the fact that many things in life are evil, and must be said to be evil. They are to be resisted: not to be a ground for thanks. I prefer therefore to thank God *in* everything. Paul says in Romans 8:28, 'We know that in all things God works for good with those who love him, those whom he has called according to his purpose' (Good News Bible). If God is at work in all things, then we can thank him in all things. The distinction is crucially important, enabling us to be grateful for his presence while recognizing evil for what it is; and pointing us away from the question

20

'Your hands, Lord Jesus'
— a meditation on Luke 24:16–53

I imagine, Lord Jesus, that when you said to the two disciples, 'Peace be with you', you used your hands and the palms of your hands were facing downwards.

Later on in conversation with them, you said, 'Look at my hands and my feet' and you showed them your hands and your feet. This time the palms of your hands would be facing upwards and the disciples would see clearly the marks of the nails.

When the time of your ascension came, the Bible says that you 'raised your hands' as you returned to *your* Father — and 'Praise be' (as Thora Hird would say) to *my* Father also.

Thank you for your hands, Lord Jesus, reaching out to bless, reaching out to reveal, and reaching out to praise. Although so very inadequate, may my hands reach out to bless, to reveal and to praise.

AMEN.

A Lay Preacher

'Why did this happen to me?', and on to the question 'What might the result be of this happening to me?'

Paul is particularly grateful because of their faith, hope and love. How often these appear together in the Christian scriptures (Romans 5:5; 1 Corinthians 13; Galatians 5:5–6; Ephesians 4:2–5; 1 Thessalonians 1:3 and 5:8; Hebrews 6:10–12 and 10:22–24; 1 Peter 1:3–8 and 21–22). But they are not always in the same order. Here, for example, the hope seems to be the reason for the faith and the love. This is not too difficult to understand. 'Hope' in the New Testament is not usually thought of as a subjective condition, nor as an attitude of believing in a highly unlikely outcome. It is not 'You believe and you love because you still manage an attitude of hope'. Hope in New Testament terms has much more objective reality than that. Hope in eternal life is to accept the fact that God has already prepared eternal life for us. To hope in this sense is to await a reality which exists but which we have not yet

experienced. It is, in Paul's words here, 'Kept safe for you in heaven'. It is something to be sure of, even though you have not yet received it. And it ties in with what we read earlier in his letter about grace and peace (1:2). The 'hope of heaven' is based on the objective events of the total ministry of Christ. It has nothing to do with 'whistling in the dark'. As such, hope is a proper stimulus for faith and love.

We must also notice the comprehensiveness of the Christian vision. Faith is particularly related to the events of God's love for us in Christ in the past. Love is our current experience in the present. Hope points us forward to the ultimate fulfilment of God's purposes for us in the future. It is an exercise in tri-focalism which offers a truly broad outlook on life. We are not limited to the view of the oarsman in the boat, who sees only where he has been. Neither are we like the cox, who sees only what lies ahead. Yet neither are we like the passenger on the pleasure steamer, sitting sideways and looking at each new stretch of the bank as it appears in view. We are committed to all three — a firm foundation in what God has done in the past, a certainty that God will eventually bring all things to completion in Christ, and a present commitment to work with all our might for the kingdom now. We need that balanced breadth in our outlook, for which Paul gave thanks in relation to the Colossian Christians.

Prayer Today I thank you for so much good that comes my way, from family or friends, neighbours or those with whom I work. Then there are the happy events, the fulfilling activities, the enriching experiences. It's easy to thank you for those, though I don't do it nearly enough. Help me to take that next, very difficult, step of thanking you in the bad relationships and circumstances. I want to perceive your grace at work in those too; not in *causing* them (though you must be *allowing* them) but in using them for good to me or others. In the Spirit let me hope, believe and love.

Lent 1/Wednesday   Colossians 1:5

. . . the faith and love that spring from the hope that is stored up for you in heaven and that you have already heard about in the word of truth, the gospel that has come to you.

'The word of truth'

In the middle of Paul's thanksgiving in yesterday's passage, there appears the phrase selected for today: 'the word of truth'. Paul is referring to the time when Christian preachers first brought the message to Colossae. It is important to notice why he describes the gospel message as the word of truth.

In the Colossian situation the major reason for referring to truth was that heresy seemed to be flourishing. Judging from Paul's references to the false teaching being propounded at Colossae, it was an early form of what later came to be known as gnosticism. We shall look at different parts of that teaching as we go through this letter. For the moment we need simply to observe that the false teaching demeaned the stature of Christ and misrepresented the meaning of salvation. In simple language, it was wrong.

Paul needs therefore to remind his readers that, by contrast with this heresy, the gospel is 'the word of truth'.

We do well to ponder this point in our contemporary setting, too. We live in days when relativism still exercises considerable influence. Absolute and universal values are not honoured: everything depends on the context and the demand of the moment. Parallel with that outlook there is an easy-going tolerance which encourages us to select what we find most acceptable. So we hear people saying, 'That may be true for you, but it isn't true for me'. There is, of course, a wide range of life's experiences where this is not only acceptable, but necessary. Where such attitudes are dangerously misleading is at the level of fundamental values and assumptions, because they undermine the fabric of life itself. The question of truth is one such level.

We need to beware of this warning in our modern church life too. In the past two decades there has been a much needed return in confidence about Christian experience. Charismatic renewal with its emphasis on the fulness, fruit and gifts of the Spirit has had a considerable influence. Liturgical renewal, with its high profile for sacramental expressions of the faith, has also influenced many. Both forms of new life have brought added focus on worship, spirituality and the place of sensibility in Christian belief. The reaction against over-cerebral faith is now in danger of becoming a neglect of the mind in faith, and this will be disastrous. The mind is vital if the truth of the faith is to be safeguarded.

In the end, the fundamental reason for being a Christian is that it is true. What we feel and what we do are, of course, important; but neither carry much weight if at their heart the received message is not true.

Concern for truth naturally raises questions of doctrine, of the content of what is believed. Here the sensitive understanding of the Bible, some grasp of basic doctrine, and a willingness to 'think things through' are vital. No amount of feeling and doing can make up for failure in that task. All three are needed, but it is the question of truth that is basic.

Paul says that the Colossians 'received the word of truth'. This puts the use of the mind into proper perspective, too. Christianity is not a faith where the intellectual is automatically outstanding. Whatever information we gain, whatever knowledge we have, whatever doctrine we learn, the truth has to be received into our lives by faith.

The basis of Christian believing is what God did in history through Jesus Christ. This is the central content of the faith, the basis of everything else. Its truth is therefore fundamental. If it is true, then feelings and actions must harmonize with that truth. This is part of the obedience of faith. Once we begin to neglect truth-questions, we are threatening the whole structure of believing. The message of the gospel is the word of truth.

Prayer I could give you lots of reasons why I believe in you, Lord! Don't let me forget the simplest reason of all — that you are true. It's easy to be carried along on a wave of feelings or actions, but that's like building a house on sand if there isn't a foundation of truth at the base. So help me today to reflect on the truth of that gospel, and particularly on Jesus Christ as the way, the truth and the life. And let my life 'ring true' in harmony with his.

Lent 1/Thursday   Colossians 1:6–8

All over the world this gospel is bearing fruit and growing, just as it has been doing among you since the day you heard it and understood God's grace in all its truth. You learned it from Epaphras, our dear fellow-servant, who is a faithful minister of Christ on our behalf, and who also told us of your love in the Spirit.

God . . . Christ . . . Spirit

Paul is still describing the Christian experience of his readers of Colossae, as it had been reported to him by Epaphras. He rejoices that they have 'understood the grace of God'. He praises Epaphras as a 'faithful minister of Christ'. He says Epaphras has told him of their 'love in the Spirit'.

In these highly experiential days, it is natural to note the emphasis on grace, faithfulness and love. A much deeper issue is uncovered in these three verses, however. It is the trinitarian nature of God as Father, Son and Spirit. It has often been said that there are only hints of a doctrine of the Trinity in the Old Testament, and that there is no developed, consistent trinitarian doctrine in the New Testament. I believe this makes the case for trinitarian belief even stronger.

We need to begin by remembering that the Jewish faith, the soil in which the seeds of Christianity were planted, was sharply monotheistic. It was this belief in one God that distinguished Israel from the other nations throughout her history. The earliest Christians had been trained from youth to recite, 'The Lord our God, the Lord is one'. They were not prepared for a trinitarian understanding.

The idea of trinity did not come to them first as a tenet of belief, however. It came as an experience. The Jews who followed Jesus tried to place him in their human categories. In the end Peter was faced with the direct question by Jesus and blurted out, 'You are the Christ, the Son of the living God'. He was not chastised by Jesus for saying this. Rather he was praised (Matthew

25

16:17). They were beginning to grasp that the only way to understand who Jesus was would be to allow the category of deity to be part of the description. They were on the way to a two-person concept of God (not as people but as forms of the God-head). John's Gospel makes it clear that barely had they begun to grasp this insight when Jesus told them he was going away. When sadness showed on their faces he comforted them by promising that they would not be alone because he would send them 'another counsellor', and the word 'another' means 'another of the same sort' (John 16:16). When, on the Day of Pentecost and afterwards, the Holy Spirit came upon the disciples, they recognized that 'the other' had come (Acts 2). In the rest of the Acts, where Luke describes the results of the Spirit's presence, and in the New Testament letters where the work of the Spirit is described, it becomes increasingly clear that what the Spirit does among the Christians is to make the meaning of Christ clear in their minds, the presence of Christ strong in their lives, and the works of Christ plentiful in their witness. The Spirit makes the church the community of the words and works of Jesus. They experience and witness to God, through Jesus, by the Spirit. Since they encounter deity at each of these poles of their daily life, Trinity becomes the way to understand God. Whether as Father, Son or Spirit, it is the same God they meet. Yet their experience of each has been different in terms of time, occasion and result.

It is for this reason that it is so natural that here in Colossians Paul does not deliberately set out a formal doctrine of the Trinity. He is describing the Christian experience of his readers, and each member of the God-head is mentioned in turn. That is how the earliest Christians had discovered God to be. It is how we are likely better to understand him too.

C. S. Lewis illustrated this point beautifully when he found praying to be a trinitarian experience. We come to God the Father, in the name of Christ the Son, through the power of the Holy Spirit the Counsellor. And that is authentic meaningful Christian experience.

Prayer Father, Son and Holy Spirit, I don't find the doctrine of the Trinity easy to believe! I certainly don't understand it. 'Three in one and one in three' is brief and memorable: but it's also mathematically impossible. Yet I do see that the disciples could describe Jesus adequately only in terms of their heavenly Father's Son. And I understand why they felt, on the Day of Pentecost, that the Holy Spirit was doing through them what Jesus had done. I'd like to follow that way, too, today, knowing God, through Jesus by the Spirit; and letting my understanding grow within the experience.

You learned it from Epaphras, our dear fellow-servant, who is a faithful minister of Christ on our behalf.

Epaphras

We are now introduced to a second individual involved with the Christian church at Colossae — called Epaphras. He is one of the group of people whose names we read in the New Testament, but about whom we know comparatively little. Yet they must have been vital to the growth and development of the early church.

Some things are clear about Epaphras. Paul, writing to the Colossians, says that Epaphras is 'one of you'. One assumes that means that Epaphras was 'a local boy' who has become a recognized evangelist. Paul seems never to have been to Colossae, and therefore had to rely on people like Epaphras for his knowledge of the Colossian situation and church. So in 1:18 Paul says that Epaphras has 'made known to us your love in the Spirit'. He has also played his part in building up the Colossian church. In 1:7 it was he who 'brought the good news, who preached the Word of truth'. So he was both their teacher in the faith, and the one who went between Paul and the Christians he had never met. Paul now writes to them precisely because of the report about them from Epaphras.

We discover a great deal about the life of the church if we pause to reflect on the importance in the early days of people like Epaphras. How many names of the early Christian leaders do you know? When you move beyond Paul, Peter, perhaps James, where do you go? Epaphras, Timothy, Barnabas, Ananias, Mark? How much do you know about them? Very little. Yet this second line of people was absolutely crucial in the life of the church. Paul's work probably could not have been done without such people. How many were there in the next few circles out from the centre, of whom we know nothing at all?

Part of the value of the concept of the church as the body of Christ is that it underlines the importance of every limb and organ. Their significance is to be measured, not by their worth in comparison with what others do, but by the degree to which they do what they were fashioned to do. We in the church are far too prone to judge people's worth by their job. We glorify church leaders, great preachers, leading scholars, top administrators; often to the detriment of those who do not make headline news, yet whose work is vital to the kingdom of God. Our failure here is more serious because we live in a culture where worth is measured by job status, and therefore where the unemployed consider themselves, and are often considered to be, worthless. It is our privilege to affirm that every person is of infinite value because each is made in the image of God and so loved by God that Jesus Christ died for every one.

Christians should spell this out by their attitude to all the gifts God has given his people, not putting them into tables of merit, but thanking God for them all, equally.

We may begin that process today by remembering all those folks who helped us to faith, and giving God thanks for each in turn as we savour the memory of them before God.

Prayer First, I recall the names of those who helped me into the faith, those who built me up in it, and those who do both for me now. I surround them with an atmosphere of loving, thankful prayer. I ask to whom I could be such a helper, and how I can do that as part of my discipleship. Then I think gratefully of those who do in my church the less attractive, less honoured tasks, without whom the church couldn't continue.

Lent 1/Saturday   Colossians 1:9–14

For this reason, since the day we heard about you, we have not stopped praying for you and asking God to fill you with the knowledge of his will through all spiritual wisdom and understanding. And we pray this in order that you may live a life worthy of the Lord and may please him in every way: bearing fruit in every good work, growing in the knowledge of God, being strengthened with all power according to his glorious might so that you may have great endurance and patience, and joyfully giving thanks to the Father, who has qualified you to share in the inheritance of the saints in the kingdom of light. For he has rescued us from the dominion of darkness and brought us into the kingdom of the Son he loves, in whom we have redemption, the forgiveness of sins.

'Asking that you may be filled'

Paul now tells his readers that he has been praying for them — an interesting way of reminding them what are his own hopes for them. He begins with, 'that you may be filled'. The modern emphasis on fulness of the Spirit is often associated with the fairly recent Charismatic Renewal. We should not forget, as charismatics would remind us, that its origin is in the Bible! A reading of the Acts of the Apostles shows how significant its author, Luke, regarded it for the growth of the early Christian church. Disciples are described as being 'filled with the Spirit' as they faced particular challenges. Sometimes they are said to be 'full of the Holy Spirit', as though that were a more permanent condition. Yet even those said to be full of the Spirit can later be said to be filled with the Spirit on special occasions. The Spirit evidently operates according to laws of spiritual life rather than the laws of physics! We are all, as Christians, encouraged to be full of the Holy Spirit! In the eighteenth-century Methodist revival John Wesley in effect gave this doctrine stronger focus by encouraging the Methodist people to be 'perfected in love'. This teaching is less clear when described as 'sinless perfection', or even 'entire sanctification' though both titles can be made to fit the Wesley thought. As such John Wesley was laying upon his followers the privilege of being so controlled by divine love at the centre of their lives, that everything they said and did would flow from that one source. Since love is described in the New Testament as the first fruit of the Spirit (Galatians 5:22), and as the main gift of the Spirit (1 Corinthians 12:31–13:13), Wesley was actually underlining the fundamental principle of being totally under love's inspiration. Paul called the Colossians Christians to be filled.

The apostle then spells out what the implications will be. He prays that God will give them 'knowledge' (*gnōsis* — hence the later name, gnostic). Paul is sure that God gives freely the knowledge that his people need: there is no need for secrecy. We must not miss in our age, however, a slightly (though not wholly) different implication, for we live at a time when, rightly, education encourages us to search out everything for ourselves, rather than simply accepting what others claim to be the case. This is important for Christians, too, so long as we remember that salvation is a special area of knowledge, with particular disciplines involved. It is a special form of knowledge because by definition human minds did not invent it. Revelation was and is, therefore, necessary. And particular disciplines are needed because salvation is perceived and received by faith. Reason, understanding and human insight are vital to the process. They cannot make the knowledge complete, however, unless the truth thus commended is received by faith. The knowledge Paul commends is knowledge God gives, requiring full use of our mental faculties, but also involving our trusting response of faith in him through Jesus Christ.

This is why knowledge involves 'spiritual wisdom'. This means insight into what the kingdom is about. It is perception of how salvation could come through the death and resurrection of Jesus Christ. Paul spells this out in 1 Corinthians 1:18–31. Over against demands for signs or intellectual demonstration as proof, says Paul, the Christians preach Christ crucified. In 1 Corinthians 2, he shows what kind of wisdom this is.

He also prays for 'understanding'. By this Paul means the ability to apply their wisdom to everyday life. It is about establishing the right priorities and living by them. So much of Jesus' teaching illustrated this. Hold on to your life selfishly and you will lose what it is really about. Give your life in service of God and your fellow human beings and you will enjoy it at the deeper level. Make material possessions and status your god, and you will shrivel spiritually. Put inner purity and Christian quality as priority and you can wholly enjoy whatever little material gain you have.

The result is intended to be 'A life worthy of the Lord . . .(pleasing) him in every way: bearing fruit in every good work, growing in the knowledge of God' (1:10). It is not primarily about meetings and activities, nor even about worship, prayer or Bible, though all of these are needed. It is first and foremost about submitting our lives in service of God, being willing to serve him above all else. It is at once extremely demanding and abundantly simple.

Prayer Lord, I need help to understand what 'being filled by the Spirit' means. It does sound a bit like liquid being poured into a beaker. The idea of being 'full of love' is easier to grasp, because I've known moments like that, when love seemed to determine my whole outlook. And I remember that 'the fruit of the Spirit is love', as Paul put it. So please let your love inspire and guide everything I do today, and let that love overcome in me anything that isn't pleasing to you.

Questions for consideration by individuals or groups

1. What place has thanksgiving in the Christian life?

2. What are the implications of thinking of the gospel as 'the word of truth'?

3. How would you answer the question, 'Who is Jesus?' and how do you understand the trinitarian view of God?

'Strengthened with all power'

Our reflection on yesterday's reading may well be that it is easy to say but remarkably difficult to do. In a context where the majority are not seeking to do God's will as their prime aim, and where spiritual values are not treated with high regard, how is a Christian to put service of the Lord first in life?

The answer lies in Paul's prayer that his readers 'be strengthened with all power'. There are few more important clues to living the Christian life than this one. In our western society we have tended to forget it. Under the pressure of critical scrutiny from a scientific and technological culture, raising deep questions about the thought content and the performance of Christianity, we have tended to tighten our belts and clench our fists in determination to show that one can be thoughtful and a believer, that to be a Christian does give ground for a life of integrity. All of this has been necessary, but it has also placed great emphasis on what we Christians think, say and do. It lays stress on our action rather than God's; on our understanding the situation, devising the solution, and acting accordingly. As such it is in danger of misconstruing the nature of Christianity altogether.

We are not primarily Christians because we found God. He found us. In larger terms he took the initiative in the life, death, resurrection and ascension of Jesus. But for that there would be no Christianity. That is the fundamental initiative. Everything we do is response. This is what our sacraments make abundantly plain. 'We love' says John, 'because he first loved us' (1 John 4:19). Under pressure from our culture to justify being Christians, we need to hold on to this basic element in our position. After all, the distinctive feature of Christianity is not what we do. Other groups of people meet together to celebrate, hold discussions on topics of mutual interest, organize through a variety of committees, and engage in caring activity. If there is anything different about Christianity it is the reality of the existence of God revealed in Jesus Christ, a God who is in the midst of his people. One of our major differences should therefore be that of having God's sustaining power in our lives. We do not simply believe in the truth about God; we receive power by the grace of God.

A parallel passage in Ephesians (1:19–20) spells out what kind of power that is. It is the power by which God raised Jesus from the dead. Part of our privilege as people born again by God's Spirit is to know the presence of resurrection power in our lives. I sometimes wonder whether we Christians are deflected from the truth through some of our own systems. We are encouraged to go to worship because we need the help it affords. We have

31

intricate systems of fellowship and formal counselling set up. Charismatic emphasis upon the variety of caring skills and on body ministry strengthens the network of dependence. Of course these emphases are right, and God does work through them to help us. Far more important than any of these, however, is God's work within each of our lives, by which alone we are able to take part in and benefit from our worship, fellowship, counselling and ministry. Too many Christians are neither as fulfilled nor as effective as they could be, because they have not fully explored the implication of having resurrection power in their lives.

Paul says such power produces, for example, 'endurance' and 'patience' (1:11). Endurance here is particularly connected with circumstances. Patience relates especially to people. As the late L. B. Caird put it, 'Endurance is the refusal to be daunted by hard times, patience is the refusal

to be upset by perverse people'. In a culture where everything is 'instant' — food, shopping, information, sex — we do well to remember that God is steadily building Christian character in his people, accompanied by 'joy'.

The patient endurance of the Christian gospel in the world is one of its most endearing qualities. When people were saying that Christianity was coming to an end, many were dedicating their lives to producing the beautiful artistic presentations of the Gospels, known as the Book of Kells. It is a continuing testimony to the many judgements on the prophets of doom. Voltaire once wrote, 'When my works have gone round the world, the Bible will be a forgotten book'. The house in Paris where he wrote these words later became a distributing centre of the British and Foreign Bible Society!

Prayer I live in a world where power is greatly valued. It does have so many forms — political power, economic power, military power. I hardly seem to be in that league, Lord. Even your church as a whole seems to come off badly in such company. Power is not the word you'd choose first to describe the local congregation. Help me to remember that it wasn't the word you would have used of the dead, crucified Jesus, either. Yet he rose to change the whole course of history. Enlarge my thoughts and deepen my spirit so that I can comprehend and experience more fully the truth that resurrection power dwells in me through my faith in Jesus. Then let me dare to change my bit of the world for him.

Lent 2/Monday   Colossians 1:12–14

. . . giving thanks to the Father, who has qualified you to share in the inheritance of the saints in the kingdom of light. For he has rescued us from the dominion of darkness and brought us into the kingdom of the Son he loves, in whom we have redemption, the forgiveness of sins.

Redemption

Paul's assumption, in his prayer for the Colossians, is that they will joyfully give thanks to God, even in the midst of endurance and patience. It is an interesting fact of New Testament teaching that the word 'joy' almost always occurs in the context of pain, hardship, suffering or persecution. In other words it is not easily associated with what we mean by the word 'happy'. It certainly is not something dependent on our circumstances either. It is a deeper level of gladness than that. It is possible to have joy in sorrow, in pain, in hardship because it springs from 'gladness in God'. It does not focus on how we feel, or on how things are, or on our hope for a brighter future. Joy originates in the presence of God at the heart of our lives, through tears or smiles, good days or bad, health or illness. That is why it is sometimes referred to as 'joy in the Lord'.

Here Paul associates joy with thankfulness (1:12). They can thank God for the change he has brought about in their lives. To make clear what change is he uses two contrasts, light and darkness and two kinds of kingdom.

The kingdom contrast shows that the change brought about by becoming a Christian is a change in fundamental allegiance. A major factor in the life of the kingdom is the loyalty of the subjects to their monarch. Paul does not here say who is the king of the 'dominion of darkness' (1:13). We can guess from some of his other writings, however. Perhaps he does not mention that tyrant because he wishes to concentrate on the nature of the other kingdom, obedience to the Father and 'to the Son he loves' (1:12–13). The images are the very opposite of the tyrannical. 'The Father to the Son he loves' could hardly be more warm, affirming and welcoming. Paul intends a contrast here with the false teaching of Colossae which saw salvation as a process passing through different spiritual beings until finally reaching the ultimate God. How different that process is from the welcome given by a father to the son he loves! Who would not wish to belong to that kingdom? It declares the universe to be, at its heart, personal. It elevates relationships to the highest level in our existence. It points the way to meaning in life via personal, family categories. If this kingdom involves obedience, then it is obedience to the law of love.

The depth of that is shown by the process which enables us to enter the kingdom, redemption involving the forgiveness of sins. The word 'redemption' or 'ransom' was used in the Graeco-Roman world, as its Hebrew equivalent had been used in Old Testament times. Put simply it means 'the price paid to set you free', often from death. It is also used as the price paid to free someone from slavery. The New Testament does not ask or answer the question, 'To whom was the price paid?' That is not the point of the metaphor. The emphasis is on the costliness of the payment (see Romans 5:6–8, for example) and the wonderful result (see Romans 5:9–11). In Jesus Christ God has shown that his love goes even through death so that we might be set free from sin's control, and lead new lives.

This is the point of the second contrast, darkness and light. The challenge of obedience leads to a change of prevailing atmosphere in our lives. The dark throngs of evil are to be left behind. We are moving into the light of what is good, lovely and true. This is the basic meaning of baptism, dying with Christ and all that is dark; rising with Christ to all that is light. And God has made all this possible through Jesus Christ.

It is said that in a Nazi concentration camp, when women were being lined up for extermination, a nun took the place of a little girl. How does that little girl feel about such an act of love which set her free? How do we feel about the far greater act of love with which the Son of God set us free?

Prayer I thank you, O God, that my life is different from what it might be, because I belong to your kingdom, and because I'm committed to walking in the light and not the darkness. I'm overwhelmed by the reminder that at the centre of that change in my life is the dying of Jesus Christ, the ransom which sets me free. That puts a high price on my freedom and salvation. I want to live with the dignity and dedication that befit such costly redemption.

Lent 2/Tuesday   Colossians 1:15–20

He is the image of the invisible God, the firstborn over all creation. For by him all things were created: things in heaven and on earth, visible and invisible, whether thrones or powers or rulers or authorities; all things were created by him and for him. He is before all things, and in him all things hold together. And he is the head of the body, the church; he is the beginning and the firstborn from among the dead, so that in everything he might have the supremacy. For God was pleased to have all his fulness dwell in him, and through him to reconcile to himself all things, whether things on earth or things in heaven, by making peace through his blood, shed on the cross.

He is. . .

Paul now comes to the meat of the theological argument against the false teachers of Colossae. They seem to have taught that there was a kind of stairway to God, with spiritual beings on each step, by whom one made one's progress to the ultimate God. They may even have placed Jesus Christ somewhere in this series of approach beings. The apostle has already argued that redemption is God's work, through Jesus Christ alone, 'the Son he loves' (1:13). Now he must explain why he puts Christ into this unique position. Hence the repetition, throughout the passage, of the words 'He is. . . '

'He is the image of the invisible God.' The words 'image of God' were, of course, used of other human beings in the Bible (Genesis 1:26; 1 Corinthians 11:7; 2 Corinthians 3:18; Colossians 3:10). But two things are different here. He is the image of the 'invisible' God; stressing a revelation of what is otherwise nowhere to be seen. And as Paul claims later, in Christ all God's fulness dwells (1:19). He not only reveals of God what no one else reveals, he is also within himself a total revelation of what God is, could we but perceive it. This is the given foundation on which all Christianity is built.

He is the 'first-born of all creation'. This could mean created like everyone else, only earlier. But the word used really means, at root, 'prior'. We apply it naturally as 'prior in time', that is, 'earlier'. But it came increasingly to mean 'prior in importance', that is 'superior'. This meaning fits everything else that Paul writes about Jesus Christ. As one translation puts it, 'His is the primacy over all created beings'.

'For by him all things were created.' This is a recurring theme, in different parts of the New Testament (Colossians 1:16, Hebrews 1:2; John 1:3). Fundamental to this insight is the idea that what God revealed in Jesus Christ is the clue to the purpose of the whole universe. Love, healing, spirituality, inwardness, self-giving, awe and patience are the kind of qualities around which our world is meant to work. Without them no major world issues will ever be solved.

Paul's specific point here is that all the beings and authorities to which the false teachers referred — if they had any existence at all — also owe their origin to Christ. He must be superior to them. What is more, the consistency of the universe owes its origin to him, too. Paul claims that, 'in him all things hold together' (1:17).

These are deep matters, but a more demanding idea comes next. 'He is the head of the body, the church' (1:18). This one, of whom such high theology has been expounded, is also linked to the church as a head to a body. It is this which gives the church its dignity and its mystery. He who is the key to the whole created universe is also the key to the church. For Christians he is both the source of life and the assurance of resurrection ('the beginning and the firstborn from among the dead' 1:18).

Paul's point is now driven home again. 'So that in everything he might have the supremacy. For God was pleased to have all his fulness dwell in him' (1:18–19). He means that there can be no religion superior to Christianity, since the fulness of God dwelt in Jesus Christ. 'Fulness' seems to have been a word used by the false teachers. Paul says the fulness dwelt in Christ.

Most moving of all is Paul's last claim in this section. This comprehensive person, Jesus Christ, who is the clue to the existence of both the universe and the church, gave his life on the cross in order to reconcile everything to God.

The implications of this passage are enormous. We must not narrow down our understanding of Christ to individual, pietist categories: he is the clue to all the world, so his people must have a vision as wide as the world. Yet the world is not automatically saved because he is its clue. Christ is head of the church so that, as his body, it may witness to salvation. And that salvation is found in the death of Jesus Christ. The aim is to reconcile all things to God, and we can play our part in that mission to the world.

Prayer At this point, Father, I have to confess that I'm getting out of my depth! It isn't easy to clothe these descriptions of Jesus with matter-of-fact meanings. They are much too profound. But I can see that the world would be a better place if what he stood for was central in the affairs of the world. And I do know that there is a genuine experience of forgiveness through his death. That he should be head of the church is perhaps the greatest miracle of all. I am so grateful for everything he is and does.

Lent 2/Wednesday   Colossians 1:21–23

Once you were alienated from God and were enemies in your minds because of your evil behaviour. But now he has reconciled you by Christ's physical body through death to present you holy in his sight, without blemish and free from accusation — if you continue in your faith, established and firm, not moved from the hope held out in the gospel. This is the gospel that you heard and that has been proclaimed to every creature under heaven, and of which I, Paul, have become a servant.

Continue faithful

Lest his readers should have any idea that Christ as the clue to creation and redemption means that all are automatically saved, Paul now reminds them of their own story (1:21–22). Once God was not the centre of their lives. In awareness, in deed and in thought they were actually moving away from him. In a world where God is present there is actually no neutrality. We either respond to his presence and move towards it, or we live as though it was not there and move away from it. Paul's readers had once been in the latter state. He can even call them God's enemies. Life in an exciting secular environment may tend to mask that truth in the awareness of many people. And after all, lots of people live like that. But the fact is that not to serve him is to oppose his presence and purpose in the world. There is much talk about alienation in our world — alienation from work, from life, from one another. The root of all alienation is at a much more basic level, alienation from the God who made us and gave us all that we have. Once we are out of step there — alienated from God and his plan for his world — all other forms of alienation are not only likely, they are predictable. Till the source of the disease is dealt with the spots will keep appearing on the skin, however much ointment we apply.

A PRAYER/POEM

Only a seed lying alone,
Down in the cold dark earth;
Waiting, watching patiently
For God's new birth.

Only a seed coming alive
Fed by the sun and the rain;
Growing, growing, tall and strong
Coming to life again.

Only me, Lord, waiting for you,
Watching and praying — that I have the strength —
To do all that you have planned for me.
HERE! NOW! You have given *me* new life!

AMEN.

An adult church leader

The piece of music by Dukas, called 'The Sorcerer's Apprentice' depicts the young helper trying to take over in his master's absence. He has heard the expert start everything in motion and he uses that knowledge to begin to set objects around him moving — tables and chairs, brushes and buckets, furniture and ornaments. As one listens to the music one recognizes the growing excitement of this young man's sense of power. As the music grows in volume, however, one hears the first indication of doubt as a new question emerges. He has started everything going. Can he either control or stop it? The music tells us he can not. From now on we move from harmony, through pandemonium towards chaos till the master returns and brings everything under control. It is a parable of much of our modern life. We have a vast range of energies, skills and knowledge, all given by God. Yet the scale of threat, injustice, mistrust rises steadily, till the possible end-point of chaos becomes almost inevitable. We need again to be under the hand of the master.

But all is not lost. Paul reminds them again that God's self-giving in Christ has introduced a wholly new way for us to follow; the way of holiness, purity, faultlessness (1:22). It is a road along which all may travel by faith in Christ, gratefully receiving life's gifts and gladly using them according to the purpose of the giver for good in the world.

There is a condition. The tri-focal element enters in again. There is a firm and sure foundation in God's work for us in the life, death, resurrection and ascension of Jesus Christ. On that foundation we are to build. There is a hope for the future in God's promise of the establishing of his kingdom. Towards the future we are to move. Here and now we are to continue faithful, working out the implications for our lives of the past foundations as future hope.

For Paul it means becoming 'a servant of the gospel'. It will mean that for each one of us, too, though not in the same way as for Paul. We might sum up the challenges by answering the question posed by an American preacher: 'What is there about your life that requires Jesus Christ as the explanation?'

Prayer Lord, I am sometimes frightened by what I see and hear happening in the world. There is brash confidence about what human beings can yet do; but there are unmistakable signs of imminent disaster, too. In that setting it isn't always easy to remain faithful, because so many around me seem not to care. Yet I remember what life would be without you. I recall too the foundation you laid in the ministry of Christ, as well as the hope we have for the future. On the strength of those I commit myself afresh for faithful discipleship in the world.

Lent 2/Thursday   Colossians 1:24

Now I rejoice in what was suffered for you, and I fill up in my flesh what is still lacking in regard to Christ's afflictions, for the sake of his body, which is the church.

'I rejoice in what was suffered for you'

Paul has been reminding his readers of their testimony. Now he tells them something of his. 'I rejoice in my sufferings' is not easy to believe. We saw earlier how often joy and suffering go together in the New Testament. Here it is again. I expect he is referring primarily to being in prison, but he might have in mind the wider list of life's hardships, set out in 2 Corinthians 11:23–29. Paul really did go through the mill for his faith and his calling. It is a far cry from those who teach that if you are faithful God makes sure that you prosper in circumstances and possessions. Why could anyone go through such suffering, let alone rejoice in it?

First, because it is for the sake of fellow Christians. He says it is, 'For your sake'. The logic of the argument seems to be that anyone who proclaims God's word in an unsympathetic context will pay the price for doing so. Since he preaches in order that his hearers should benefit, then his sufferings truly are for the sake of the hearers. But, we recall, Paul had never been to Colossae, and being in prison he had little hope of doing so. How could Paul's sufferings be for their sakes?

The answer is probably that Paul is thinking more naturally in collective terms than we do in our individualistic culture. Wherever suffering is endured for the gospel, it is borne on behalf of all those who benefit from the gospel. The good news of Jesus brings blessing and pain, and they belong to the body of Christ. If I enjoy the benefits of the gospel, then those at present who suffer for the gospel are suffering for my sake. Those who are imprisoned, persecuted, mocked or discriminated against for the sake of the gospel are, by their share in that gospel experience, making my gospel experience possible. Paul suffers in prison and is glad that his readers benefit.

But there is a deeper and far more searching reason. Paul writes 'I fill up in my flesh what is still lacking in regard to Christ's afflictions' (1:24). We need to pause in awe before that claim. He cannot mean that what he goes through is part of that suffering by which our salvation was provided, for we know from elsewhere that Paul did not believe that. He is adamant that our redemption is through Christ alone.

Yet there is a sharing in Christ's sufferings in two ways. One is that by our baptism — signified through the earliest experience of adult believers being plunged into a river or sea — we are identified with Christ in his suffering and resurrection. In that sense every Christian will go through suffering at some time or other for their faith. In that way, so long as there are more people yet to become Christians, there are more of the sufferings of Christ to be made up.

There may be a second meaning, however, related to the experience of people like Paul. Christ's death and resurrection were not isolated incidents happening to one person. They were the model for the entire struggle of good and evil in the world. Wherever Christ's way is followed, death and resurrection will be present. Where people, like Paul, are the spearhead of such action, the suffering will be most clear, and possibly most severe.

A third reason, perhaps a generalization from the first, is that the suffering is for the sake of the church seen as Christ's body. This very intimate way of describing the community of believers brings the two kinds of suffering together. Christ's atoning death brought the church into being. Members of the church, seen as his body, now share his sufferings in order that more may receive the good news. Suffering for others is a characteristic of the family of God.

In Melbourne, Australia, I visited a large park on a Sunday afternoon. At one point a memorial service was being held for the 'Desert Rats', members of Montgomery's army whose victory virtually won the second world war. Less than a quarter of a mile away was a huge 'pop' concert. The hundreds of young people there were oblivious to the fact of the memorial service or its meaning. Yet their freedom to sit in the sun listening to the music was won by those who were being commemorated, who gave their lives.

Pastor and Mrs Richard Wurmbrand once stayed in our house. It was a deeply moving experience to have at one's table people who had suffered so much in order that their understanding of the gospel might not be lost. Remember today those who suffer for their faith. In another sense they suffer for us. Thank God for their courage and join them in spirit today, seeking to share their burden in your prayers.

Prayer I don't remember being told much about the sufferings of a Christian when I was first coming into the faith. There was a lot about Christ's suffering, but very little about ours. Yet it's obvious when I think about it. To join Christ is to enter the battle against evil in the world, and you can't fight a battle without risk of being hurt. Thank you that my suffering is nothing like Christ's, and yet he graciously joins mine to his. Thank you that my suffering for the faith will benefit others. Thank you that so many are willing to suffer that I may have the freedom to believe.

Lent 2/Friday   Colossians 1:25–27

I have become its servant by the commission God gave me to present to you the word of God in its fulness — the mystery that has been kept hidden for ages and generations, but is now disclosed to the saints. To them God has chosen to make known among the Gentiles the glorious riches of this mystery, which is Christ in you, the hope of glory.

'The mystery . . . kept hidden'

Paul now introduces another reason why he is willing to bear suffering, though it is one removed from the other reasons. It is that he is a servant of the church, Christ's body, by a commission from God himself. If suffering comes, then it is in the cause of fulfilling his commission. We pause simply to note that 'servant' could be translated 'minister' — a warning to those formally known as 'ministers', lest we think too highly of ourselves. Haughty or proud ministers are a contradiction in terms.

What is the commission? It is 'to present to you the word of God in its fulness' (1:25). Emphasis upon the word is a healthy reminder, in these days of activism and social concern, that the New Testament constantly explains the need to proclaim the good news, and to explain godly actions. The Christian deeds presented a question to be answered. The preaching of the word provided the answer.

It is significant, too, that the word was preached in its fulness. Since the false teachers boasted of a fulness of knowledge, Paul has already reminded them of the fulness of the Godhead in Christ (1:19). Now he affirms the fulness of the word of the gospel proclaimed. If divine fulness is in Christ, why would all these extra spiritual beings be needed? If the preached word of the gospel has fulness, how could the heretics claim to add something further?

The message may be full, yet it is described as a 'mystery' (1:16). This word does not mean what we understand by a mystery, something puzzling, veiled or unclear. It means rather 'that which has been hidden but which is now revealed'. Paul writes that it 'has been kept hidden for ages and generations, but is now disclosed to the saints' (1:26). Two points emerge from such a description. One is that the Old Testament story is really an account of God's preparation for the coming of Jesus. Creation, exodus, covenant, sacrifice, priesthood, prophecy, kingship, were the core of the experience of the Israelites. They found their consummation in Jesus Christ. How long and patiently God prepared! How impatient we often are!

The other reflection from these words is that God did not become a loving father able to forgive his erring children, from the ministry of Jesus onwards. Rather the ministry of Jesus revealed what had always been true of God, that he is a loving father who forgives. The ministry of Jesus was an enactment on the stage of life of the drama that is always true of God. He has always been a 'dying-and-rising-in-Jesus-Christ God'.

The wonder of this generosity in the heart of God is now made abundantly plain. The mystery is that this grace includes Gentiles as well as Jews (1:27). 'Christ in you, the hope and glory' is a message preached to all. As Charles Wesley triumphantly wrote,

'For all, for all my Saviour died,

For all, for all was crucified'.

It is not easy for us today (most of us Gentiles by this description) to grasp how difficult it was for Jewish Christians to accept the fact that God welcomed Gentiles into the kingdom. Their religion had been characterized by distinctiveness and separation from Gentiles. Now, as a whole, Gentiles may enter too, and by the same door of faith in Christ. The Jew/Gentile problem may not be ours, but in many places we have another form of the problem, where the church consists largely of one particular class, culture, race or colour. Christ's death and resurrection are meant to break down all such barriers. We need to repent often and open the way for all to receive his grace. I remember having a white South African pastor tell of a visit to a black Christian in prison. The white guard had to be present. The pastor had the communion set with him, and invited the guard to join in. He deliberately gave the bread, then the cup, first to the black man then to the white. The guard hesitated then took the cup and drank. He would never have had to do such a thing in his life before. It was a little triumph of the gospel.

Prayer Today I have to begin by being grateful that Gentiles were ever allowed into your kingdom. I have to admit that I don't often think about that. I thank you, too, that when preachers tell us that the gospel is a mystery they don't mean it's difficult, but rather that what was hidden is now revealed. I'm glad that what was revealed was meant to break all barriers down, so please help me to treat all other people for what they are, fellow human beings with at least as much worth as I have.

Lent 2/Saturday   Colossians 1:28–29

We proclaim him, admonishing and teaching everyone with all wisdom, so that we may present everyone perfect in Christ. To this end I labour, struggling with all his energy, which so powerfully works in me.

'Present everyone perfect in Christ'

The emphasis on all that God has done, is doing and will do for us should not lull us into false security or indolence. The knowledge of the gospel is itself an incentive to tell others. The reason for making the good news known is that it *is* good news. So Paul says, 'We proclaim him'. One of John Wesley's oft-repeated journal entries was, 'I offered them Christ'.

This is no easy repetition of formalized statements, however. It involves 'admonishing' and 'teaching'. The word admonishing is included because the gospel judges those areas of our lives which are out of harmony with God's purposes. Like the music teacher striking the correct note at the end of an unaccompanied song by the choir, showing how out of tune it was, so the message about Jesus is a constant reminder of what our lives ought to be like. Paul writes in 2 Corinthians 3:18 that it is like looking into a mirror and seeing the Lord's glory, only to be turned into the likeness of that glory. He says we 'are being transformed into his likeness'. One part of that process of transformation is recognition of where we are wrong, repentance of such wrongness, and turning to the right way. So we need admonition.

We also need teaching. It is sometimes said that Christianity is 'Rather caught than taught'. I think I understand what that means. Christianity is not a class-room religion, learned like some set of lessons and reproduced in examinations. There is about it a commitment of oneself which is vital. All that I gladly accept. But it is even more important that if nothing is taught there will be nothing to be caught! Christianity is not a mood passed on, an atmosphere transposed from place to place. It is about something which God did in Jesus Christ, by which he made clear what he is like for all eternity. To be a Christian is to perceive something of what God was doing in Jesus, to respond to it by faith, and then to live one's life in service of Christ. This means that the need for teaching is paramount.

It is not simply a reciting of facts, however. Paul says that he teaches 'with all wisdom'. That brings us back to the idea of perceiving meaning of life in relation to what Christ said and did. I once heard a preacher describe how, at the age of six, he received a Christmas annual. The centre spread was a two-page picture with the title 'Look carefully — what do you see?' He was insulted by the caption; the picture was a busy farmyard with all the necessary components. Later, however, he looked at it again and saw that all those parts of the farmyard scene actually composed a lion's head. Once he saw that, he found it hard to believe that he had ever thought of it as a farmyard. The wisdom of Christian teaching is the meaning of what God was doing in Christ.

Even that is not the end. The aim of admonishing and teaching is perfection, or maturity, in Christ. Too many Christians are satisfied with a certain level of insight, knowledge and effectiveness. They settle with that before the going becomes too demanding. Paul says that he labours, struggling to lead people on to maturity. The strength to do so is given for, Paul says, it is due to 'his energy, which so powerfully works in me'. Paul, like the rest of us, is impotent without divine power working in him.

Our birthdays, anniversaries, communion services provide opportunities to ask ourselves again whether we are still going on towards maturity. Those of us with pastoral responsibility need to be sure that we are leading our people there.

Prayer I can't deny, Lord, that it is very tempting to settle in at one's present level of Christian growth and to try to coast along. So I'm glad to have this prodding from the admonition and teaching of the gospel. The aim of full maturity in Christ is exciting, too. There's nothing I'd like better. Thank you for the divine energy which makes it possible. May that same divine energy enable me properly to play my part.

Questions for consideration by individuals or groups

1. How would you explain the difference it makes to be a Christian?

2. How would you explain the Christian understanding of redemption to a non-Christian?

3. What do you see as the place of suffering in the Christian life?

I want you to know how much I am struggling for you and for those at
Laodicea, and for all who have not met me personally. My purpose is that
they may be encouraged in heart and united in love, so that they may have
the full riches of complete understanding, in order that they may know the
mystery of God, namely, Christ, in whom are hidden all the treasures of
wisdom and knowledge. I tell you this so that no-one may deceive you by
fine-sounding arguments. For though I am absent from you in body, I am
present with you in spirit and delight to see how orderly you are and how firm
your faith in Christ is.

'That no-one may deceive you'

Paul now wishes to sum up the first part of his letter. It has dealt with his
relationship to his readers, the incomparability of God's offer of salvation in
Jesus Christ, and the experience of the Colossian Christians as a result. He
has also told them what he hopes will be their pattern of growth. Soon he will
be turning to deal with the false teaching at Colossae, but he pauses to drive
home the points already made.

He has never met them, but he still 'struggles' for them. The Greek word
translated 'struggle' gives us our English word 'agony'. He is describing a
mixture of serious concern and energetic prayer on their behalf. This 'travail
of the soul' for other Christians is vital in the spiritual struggle. Effectiveness
in pastoral care probably owes more to this hidden factor than to any other
part of the pastor's work.

He wants them to be 'encouraged in heart' (2:2). The ravages of false
teaching included the unsettling of the believers. 'Heart' here carries the
meaning of will and spirit. He does not wish their resolve to be undermined,
nor their confidence. The Christian life is not an endless debating society,
trying out each new idea in a detached and relaxed atmosphere. Paul met
that attitude in Athens when invited to speak to the Areopagus there. Luke
says they 'spent their time doing nothing but talking about and listening to
the latest ideas' (Acts 17:21). Paul spoke to them in terms they understood
(Acts 17:22ff), but his challenge contrasted with their attitude. God, he told
them, 'now commands all people everywhere to repent' (Acts 17:30).
Salvation is too important a matter for endless speculation. We have to make
up our minds and resolutely follow through our commitment.

Paul also longs for them to be 'united in love' (Colossians 2:2). If
irresolution undermines faith, so does disunity. His word translated 'unified'
really means 'knit together', and he probably has in mind again the unity of a
human body — tissues, ligaments, tendons, nervous system all joined

together under the control of the brain. But it is a unity of *love*. There is nothing automatic about it. What Paul wants will only grow out of Christ-like loving, forgiving, caring attitudes between Christians being turned into words and actions.

On the basis of this encouragement and unity they can discover 'complete understanding' (2:2). The word means 'assured knowledge', and has about it the idea of someone convinced enough about something not to need constantly to question it again, but able to build on what he or she knows. False teachers will have little effect on such a person.

Encouragement, unity, assurance will lead more and more deeply into the understanding of 'the mystery of God' (2:2). Paul is now challenging the heretics on their own ground. They offered an extra, secret knowledge (*gnōsis*). He replies that Christians already have the revealed truth. It centres in Christ (2:2), 'in whom are hidden all the treasures of wisdom and knowledge'. Those who know Christ for themselves will not wish to follow false teaching for the simple reason that there is nowhere better for them to go (2:3).

Paul wants them to be able to distinguish between 'fine sounding arguments' (2:4), and the truth contained in the Christian gospel. He wants them also to know that he is present with them in spirit, and that he is impressed by what he knows of their discipline and faith.

We touch here on a crucial challenge to Christianity today. Our world, perhaps more than any other, spawns endless philosophies, systems of knowledge, new life-styles. It is easy to be caught up with one after another, becoming less and less sure about anything. Paul commends the Christian qualities of inner encouragement, corporate unity, assured knowledge and disciplined life, all focussed on Christ, as the anti-dote to an unsettling environment. We do well to 'agonize' for that in our prayers and pastoral concern for fellow Christians.

Prayer In one sense I'm in a very different situation from the readers at Colossae. They had one alternative set of ideas challenging their faiths. I face lots of such systems! Yet the way through is the same. So I ask for help to continue resolute in my commitment, in unity with my brother and sister Christians, and assured of the faith I hold. Although I don't welcome the idea, please enable me to 'agonize' in prayer about these things, for others as well as for myself.

So then, just as you received Christ Jesus as Lord, continue to live in him, rooted and built up in him, strengthened in the faith as you were taught, and overflowing with thankfulness.

'Rooted and built up'

The relationship between history and experience is set out clearly in Paul's next step in the argument. The language he uses has a technical side to it, too. The word for 'received', in 'as you received Christ Jesus as Lord', can be translated 'as you received the tradition'. Being a Christian involves the proper interrelation between what has happened in the past and what our response is now.

The tradition of 'Christ Jesus as Lord' sums up his humanity and his deity, his role as the Anointed One of God, his work as Saviour, his claim to lordship in the lives of his people. There is the tradition, the essential message. The things it describes happened whether we relate to them or not. They do not require our response, validation or confirmation. They have an objective reality of their own. They have an essential meaning of their own, too. That involves the provision of salvation for us.

Yet the objectivity of the tradition does not make our salvation inevitable. Nor does it pre-empt our response. Quite the opposite. It makes our response both reasonable and necessary. It is as we respond by faith that the objective content of the gospel message becomes subjectively meaningful for us. As we take up God's offer of salvation by committing ourselves to him, so we enter into that salvation. This is why Paul brings the tradition and the response together, in 'as you received Christ Jesus as Lord'. The content of the gospel is not determined by us: it determines the nature of our faith response. Last year I saw the Swiss Alps. Their origin and magnificence were not at all dependent on anything I did. They were 'given'. All I could do was to try to respond adequately.

This is why Paul can take the next step. He writes 'as you received Christ Jesus as Lord, continue to live in him'. The way into the faith is the way we continue to live in it, by allowing what God did in Jesus Christ to shape our response to him and to life. It is this which ought to prevent our Christianity from becoming merely internalized and individualistic, inwardly spiritual and limited to church. It involves the application to the whole of life of the truths contained in Jesus Christ. His reaching out to those whom society rejected, his concern for the poor, his healing of every part of a person, his emphasis on attitude rather than deed, his way of turning the world's

48

standards upside down, his love which set people free, his stress on self-giving as the way to happiness, his awareness of God everywhere, and his offer of forgiveness and new birth are all fundamental to the proper working of the world today. To be a Christian is to explore in experience what that means, and to commend it to others.

Paul now uses the key words to signify what that experience will be like — 'rooted', 'built up', 'strengthened', and 'overflowing'.

'Rooted' is an obvious metaphor, in an area of the world where the capacity to send down strong, deep roots was often vital if a tree or bush was to survive. The Greek tense is one which suggests an event in the past whose results go on being felt. By contrast 'built-up' is a present tense, suggesting a continuing process, the metaphor having moved from horticulture to house construction. The combination of a firm (hidden) source of stability and a growing (observable) life derived from that source, is striking.

Paul now changes metaphor again. 'Strengthened' is a legal term, which could be translated 'ratified' or 'agreed', relating as it did to the confirming of a document by both parties. It is 'what you were taught' which confirms 'your faith'. The inter-play of truth in content and authentic experience is noticeable again.

A PRAYER/POEM

Thanks be to God for this wonderful day,
Birds building nests and children at play.
Thanks be to God for the season of Spring,
The bright sunny mornings that make our hearts sing.

Thanks be to God for our homes and our friends,
The gift of true friendship that only He sends.
Thanks be to God for sunshine and showers,
The beautiful skies and wonderful flowers.

Thanks be to God for the gifts that He brings,
Thanks be to God for everything.

AMEN.

A young teenager

They are also 'overflowing', another change of metaphor. We should expect the banks of our human capacity not to be able to contain wholly the river of God's grace. So there will always be an overflowing of thankfulness.

It is the sheer sanity of Paul's outline which is so impressive. A good root, a growing faith, a deepening knowledge and a thankful attitude do not produce a bland, dull balance. They do provide a forceful steadiness.

Prayer I'm excited by this combination of metaphors Paul uses. It helps me to think of your work in Jesus Christ as the solid, life-giving earth into which my Christian roots are planted in order to spread and receive more and more sustenance. It's inspiring, too, to picture roots of faith going down and the tree of my life growing up. Let the mutual confirmation of that way of life enable me to overflow in goodness to others.

Lent 3/Tuesday   Colossians 2:8

See to it that no-one takes you captive through hollow and deceptive philosophy, which depends on human tradition and the basic principles of this world rather than on Christ.

'See to it'

Paul is now ready to take on the heretical teachers. Whatever our view of the inspiration of Scripture, it should not detract from the care with which the writers thought through what they wrote. One can almost read Paul's mind as he moves through the argument from the beginning to this point. He has reminded his readers of the rich and full heritage which is theirs in Christ through response to the orthodox gospel message. Now he will show how inferior is the alternative that they are offered in Colossae.

He begins with 'see to it', or 'look out'. It is an urgent warning. Great issues are at stake. If we imagine that being a Christian is some version of a leisure activity — how we spend some of our non-work time — then we are sadly mistaken. It is a matter of life and death, of everything or nothing, of spiritual warfare, of truth versus falsehood, of goodness versus evil. One doesn't survive in that context with a mixture of half-heartedness and carelessness. Some of us are old enough to remember a world war. How many things were explained to us with the single sentence 'There's a war on!' There were precautions to be taken, plans to be made, actions to be performed, and there

were things that were not appropriate, either, because there was a war on. It is like that all the time for the Christian. We cannot simply engage ourselves in all kinds of activity, expose ourselves to all kinds of influence, neglect those practices which deepen our spiritual perception. 'There's a war on', and we are in it!

Here Paul tells them to see to it that 'no one takes you captive'. That NIV translation is a good one. The Greek phrase is not about an animal stalking another, but about a slave trader catching a slave. Those who saw the programme 'Roots' on television will remember clearly the awful moment when the African boy Kunta Kinte found himself surrounded on his home beach by slave traders who threw over him one net after another till he was hopelessly enmeshed and unable to move. Paul warns here that false teaching can have that effect. So do not let it happen.

It is a 'hollow and deceptive philosophy' that threatens them. There is absolutely nothing wrong with philosophy as a discipline, let us hasten to affirm. After all, the word comes from two Greek words meaning the love of wisdom. There can hardly be anything wrong with that! But this particular philosophy is hollow and deceptive because, as Paul goes on, it 'depends on human tradition and the basic principles of this world rather than on Christ'.

We can now see why Paul, in verses 6 and 7, emphasized the receiving of Christ as Lord in terms of the accepting of a tradition. He wants to make the point that there are two kinds of tradition, good and bad. More precisely there is the divinely given tradition and there is the human tradition ('which depends on human tradition', 2:8). Most particularly, the distinction between the two is that the authentic tradition depends for its authenticity on Christ himself. The false tradition is according to 'the basic principles of this world' (2:8). We are here at the heart of a very deep controversy. Paul makes a similar point, though in a different context, in his first letter to the Corinthians (1:18–2:4). There he describes Jews asking for miraculous signs and Gentiles asking for wisdom but, says Paul, 'we preach Christ crucified'. He is saying that the Christian gospel about Jesus Christ cannot be fitted into any other system of thought, morality or religion. It is its own explanation and justification. It looks both weak and foolish when tested by other (worldly) systems of thought and action, yet those who enter it by faith discover it to be the power and the wisdom of God (1 Corinthians 1:18 and 30). You make your choice, enter into Christ via the gospel, and then you see how different it is from all else on offer. Do not let clever teachers lead you astray, Paul is telling his readers. And the simple, single test is, does it depend upon and honour Christ?

Prayer I have a feeling that today I am being asked to make choices. I'm being warned to be on the look out against false teaching, and I'm being reminded that there is a faithful tradition of the gospel which I should continue to guard and embrace. I'm happy with that, so long as you'll help me to perceive the difference. I'll walk with Christ.

Lent 3/Wednesday   Colossians 2:9–12

For in Christ all the fulness of the Deity lives in bodily form, and you have been given fulness in Christ, who is the Head over every power and authority. In him you were also circumcised, in the putting off of the sinful nature, not with a circumcision done by the hands of men but with circumcision done by

Christ, having been buried with him in baptism and raised with him through your faith in the power of God, who raised him from the dead.

'You have been given fulness in Christ'

There is always, when one reads the arguments from yesterday's passage, the sneaking feeling that Paul might be using a circular argument. Is Paul saying, 'You are Christians, and there cannot be anything better, so don't look at anything else and then you will increasingly know that faith in Christ is best'? Paul must be aware of that line of thought, too, so he pauses for a while to reflect with his readers on what it means to be a Christian. Are there objective as well as subjective reasons why there cannot be anything better?

His first claim is such a theological broadside that it threatens to blow the opposition off the battlefield in one shot! 'For in Christ all the fulness of the Deity lives in bodily form' (2:9). Such a claim is either true, or it is arrant nonsense. If it is true, however, the argument is virtually over from the outset.

Paul had two Greek words available to describe what is here translated 'deity'. One word means 'divine attributes', things which God can be said to be and do. The other means the 'divine essence', the very being of God himself. It is the second which Paul uses. 'The fulness of the essence of deity': it is like a phrase in Hebrews 1:3 which can be rendered 'He bears the exact reproduction of the essence of God'. How could anything be superior to that?

There is, therefore, in the proclamation of Christ, a very clear risk. One has to put to the test of each hearer and observer of the gospel this claim that fulness of deity lived in the bodily form of Christ. There is, of course, no way of proving it to others. One can simply tell the story, suggest its relevance to life today, offer one's testimony to its power in our lives, and pray that as the Holy Spirit makes the message clear, so they will be willing, helped by that same Spirit, to make a positive response. We Christians must be in no doubt that this is the crucial question. Everything else depends on a positive answer to it.

The readers at Colossae have more evidence than their judgement on the stories of Jesus, however. They have committed themselves to him, with the result that they have been gathered into the work he did in dying and rising. Paul uses two metaphors to make this clear.

One is circumcision. The Jewish practice of cutting away foreskin is used as the image of the cutting away from our lives of what is called 'your sinful nature'. It is literally 'the body of the flesh'; 'body' in the letters of Paul usually meaning the whole of a person, and 'flesh' usually meaning the whole of the person looked at from the point of view of his or her susceptibility to temptation and sin. Paul uses the picture of circumcision to make the point that becoming a Christian means setting one's whole self against all that is evil in the world, personally and in life at large. The dramatic image of cutting in circumcision is meant to show how determined and total a break this is meant to be.

The second image is baptism (2:12). Here the emphasis is not so much on us as on Christ, for Paul tells his readers that they have 'been buried with him in baptism and raised with him through your faith in the power of God, who raised him from the dead'. If the result of the first image, of circumcision, is to raise serious questions about whether we can live up to the standard involved, this second image is meant to answer the question. We are not left alone in our search for purity. Quite the opposite. It is we who are gathered into Jesus Christ's victorious struggle with evil. Our baptism signifies that as believers we are counted by God as being dead to sin and alive to new life in Christ. The God who raised Christ from the dead is the one in whose power we trust, and whose power sustains us.

These verses are the core of the letter to the Colossians. The good news is that Christ is the embodiment of deity, that his death and resurrection are the ground of our forgiveness and new life, and that believers are gathered into Christ's dying to sin and rising in power. With such an experience of salvation what else could possibly be better? Certainly not a severe system dependent on human wisdom and worldly categories. Now Paul intends us to read on!

Prayer Whenever I get into discussions about other faiths or no faiths, I always seem to end up in the same place. 'In what sense was God present in Jesus Christ?' Again and again, Father, I have to acknowledge that it makes most sense to see in him the very essence of your being. And that settles it for me. I'm glad for the image of circumcision, signifying the cutting away of all that is unworthy. And I'm grateful for baptism, too, with its assurance that because I am gathered into the death of Jesus I can also know his resurrection power. I believe it, and I claim it again for today.

Lent 3/Thursday   Colossians 2:13–15

When you were dead in your sins and in the uncircumcision of your sinful nature, God made you alive with Christ. He forgave us all our sins, having cancelled the written code, with its regulations, that was against us and that stood opposed to us; he took it away, nailing it to the cross. And having disarmed the powers and authorities, he made a public spectacle of them, triumphing over them by the cross.

'Triumphing over them by the cross'

Lest the powerful images of circumcision and baptism should not be enough, Paul now turns to another equally dramatic picture, that of debts and payments.

The word translated 'written code' in the NIV ('unfavourable record' in the Good New Bible) literally means 'bond'. It was the I.O.U. of the Graeco-Roman world. Paul says Christ took our I.O.U. and cancelled it by his death, nailing it to the cross (2:14).

But what is our I.O.U.? How are we in debt? There are two clues to the answer. One is the concept of forgiveness in 2:13 — 'He forgave us all our sins'. The key is in the words following a reference to the I.O.U., 'with its *regulations*' (2:14). It seems clear that in this image of debts and payment, the debts of Paul's readers are their failures to keep the law of God, failure to live up to his standard. The allusion to written regulations suggests that Paul has the Mosaic law in mind, but he may simply be meaning that sins are not passed over. There is a record kept.

Either way it is Paul's way of posing a problem for the heretics and answering it for the Christians. The problem is simply 'How can sinful human beings hope to approach a holy God, knowing what we are all like?' Are the false teachers able to respond to that positively, with their emphasis on secret knowledge and sets of divine beings? The Christians can, for Jesus Christ gathered all the human I.O.U.s together, carried them up with him onto the cross, and in one final act of divine love, covered all the debts, nailing the cancelled I.O.U.s to his cross. The imagery is at once masterful and breath-taking. It is complemented by the introduction of principalities and powers (2:15). They are the forces for evil, whether human or spiritual, and they occur here almost like the corporations who have goaded or tempted human beings into debt before God's law. They go away empty-handed, for Christ, on his cross, removes the debts from the scene. He triumphs over them.

An entirely different interpretation is possible. It was the custom in Roman times to put over the head of the criminal a list of the reasons for his execution. If this is prominent in Paul's mind then the implication is that, metaphorically speaking, the list of the sins of humanity was hung over Christ's head on the cross, and he bore their implications by his death. Either way, Jesus Christ is the one through whose death on the cross forgiveness and new life are available to all.

A PRAYER

Dear Lord,
Please make us think and care for those who suffer in your
world. Help us to love our neighbours and be kind to all
we know. Please help the suffering in the Continent of
Africa, especially those in Zimbabwe who we learned
about yesterday in your house. Also make us learn, pray
and serve all our lives.
We ask this in your name.

AMEN.

A Junior Missionary Collector

Not only are the principalities and powers defeated, they are humiliated. This is no small item. The point being made is not simply related to the crucifixion of Jesus. There is a principle here. Again and again as one watches world events, the power of the future tends to lie with the corporately strong — the big nations, the multi-national corporations, the big battalions. Yet in fact, the gospel affirms, their power is illusory. Far more important in life are love, peace, justice, loyalty, caring, compassion and a host of qualities which often tend to be trodden under by the onward march of the powerful. Just as the poor carpenter Messiah was crucified in loneliness yet changed the world, so in the acknowledging of God's kingdom it is the humble, the loving, the meek, the holy with whom the future lies. The imagery used is that of the Roman general coming home victorious, with the captured enemy walking in humiliation behind him. Jesus did this to principalities and powers. Is this picture of Jesus dying in our place moral? We can say with absolute conviction that it is, because we do not stand back and watch it, like spectators. When we believe we are gathered into it as participants. That is what baptism and Communion are about. Who would wish to go anywhere else?

Prayer It's unnerving to feel some responsibility for the crucifixion of Jesus Christ. Yet it's difficult to escape the logic in retrospect. Christ died to pay all the I.O.U.s, to settle all the debts, to defeat the principalities and powers. Whenever I have truck with any of that, therefore, I'm contributing to the situation which made his death necessary. I don't like that at all, but I'm so grateful that at the heart of the gospel is a word of forgiveness, not condemnation. I seek that forgiveness now, and the strength to be stronger against temptation in the future.

Lent 3/Friday   Colossians 2:16–23

Therefore do not let anyone judge you by what you eat or drink, or with regard to a religious festival, a New Moon celebration or a Sabbath day. These are a shadow of the things that were to come; the reality, however, is found in Christ. Do not let anyone who delights in false humility and the worship of angels disqualify you for the prize. Such a person goes into great detail about what he has seen, and his unspiritual mind puffs him up with idle notions. He has lost connection with the Head, from whom the whole body, supported and held together by its ligaments and sinews, grows as God causes it to grow.

Since you died with Christ to the basic principles of this world, why, as though you still belonged to it, do you submit to its rules: 'Do not handle! Do not taste! Do not touch!'? These are all destined to perish with use, because they are based on human commands and teachings. Such regulations indeed have an appearance of wisdom, with their self-imposed worship, their false humility and their harsh treatment of the body, but they lack any value in restraining sensual indulgence.

'Do not let anyone judge you'

The contrast between the profundity of the previous verses and the banality of what follows could hardly be more striking. It makes Paul's case with crushing simplicity. The choice of his readers is between being incorporated into Christ's death and resurrection or being under regulations about eating habits, observing special days, and the worship of angels. Paul knows what their choice should be!

It appears that the false teaching, apart from its rather secretive impartation of spiritual graduations to those being initiated, also contained strict rules. To judge by Paul's account of them, these regulations are not matters of individual choice: they are imposed as necessary for the different kind of salvation being offered. We today may not feel any threat from this form of gnosticism. We do well, nevertheless, to note the principles at stake which in our day have their own forms of expression and their dangers for our spirituality and discipleship. Paul's comments are salutary.

First he makes clear that questions of food, festivals and special days are not necessarily wrong. But they are shadows: not reality (2:17). What is false about the heretical teaching is that these things are counted necessary for salvation. The word 'judge' in 'do not let anyone judge you' really means 'disqualify'. Once eating customs, festivals and special days become necessary to our understanding of salvation then we are chasing shadows, not reality. Christians of every age become attracted to ways of doing things, to rules and regulations and customs which feature so highly that our eternal security seems to depend on them. Leaders who try to change our customs soon discover that! But the more we depend on these the less we depend on Christ, the reality. Be warned!

Then there is a false humility to be warned against also. It is represented by those who have special visions (in this case of the need to worship angels). At first sight they are deeply humble people, for their visions lead them into deeper abasement before more spiritual beings. In fact, says Paul, such a person comes more and more to depend on such visions as a way of gaining attention. The result is not deeper spirituality but unspiritual pride. All Christian groups stressing special gifts and visions do well to hear Paul's guidance. It is obedience in life to Christ our Head that matters, not a proliferation of impressive spiritual claims (2:19).

Thirdly Paul warns against an over-whelming emphasis on rules and regulations in the Christian life. Such systems look good and right, but only in worldly terms, Paul claims. They look wise in their orderliness, and humble in their harsh treatment of the body. In fact, however, they cannot in themselves restrain sensual indulgence (2:23). Such restraint is found elsewhere, in a recognition that we died with Christ to domination by all wordly systems and standards. It is the inner death to sin's encroachment (and inner resurrection to new life in Christ), so forcefully symbolized in baptism, that deals with sensual indulgence (2:20).

These are days, in Britain, when the Christian church is beginning to grow again. All kinds of signs of life are appearing. It is at this point that we need to hear Paul's stringent comments clearly. Our spiritual security and life depend on personal and corporate experience of Christ by our incorporation into his death and resurrection, linking our experience and God's historical acts for our salvation. This must be strongly emphasized over against all kinds of system, whether it be church organization, principles of church growth, list of unusual spiritual gifts, or new forms of worship. All such things are at best shadows: the reality is Christ. He alone is the head of the church, his body (2:19).

Prayer Lord, it isn't always easy to discern right from wrong in spiritual practices, especially when I'm caught up in the activities of the church. I think I need to be more careful about having too many rules and regulations dominating my life, taking the place of personal loyalty to Christ. Rules are easier, but they won't help me to grow spiritually if they're imposed as necessary to salvation. Grant me to live today a disciplined life that is also free.

Lent 3/Saturday   Colossians 3:1–4

Since, then, you have been raised with Christ, set your hearts on things above, where Christ is seated at the right hand of God. Set your minds on things above, not on earthly things. For you died, and your life is now hidden with Christ in God. When Christ, who is your life, appears, then you also will appear with him in glory.

'Set your hearts on things above'

The fact that Paul is not opposed to guide-lines in the Christian life, though he has warned against making too much of binding rules and regulations, is shown by the next section of his letter. Having told them where they stand in Christ, and having warned against false ideas and practices, he now wishes them to have some positive ideas about Christian growth. This is signified by his change of focal point from dying with Christ to rising with Christ (3:1). Perhaps most striking of all is his reference to Christ as now seated at God's right hand, a reminiscence from Stephen's final words as he became Christianity's first martyr, with Paul looking on. It is also another blow to the false teachers with their sets of spiritual beings. With Christ seated at God's right hand, why would we need any other way to the Father?

They are to 'set your hearts on things above' (3:1). The word translated 'set your hearts' simply means 'seek', but it is likened to the needle of the compass, 'seeking' the magnetic pole. However you steer your ship or car, the needle automatically finds magnetic north. So it should be with Christians, wherever we are put, whatever happens to us, however we are treated, we seek, like the needle, the 'things above'. But whatever does that mean?

It cannot mean that we should neglect life on earth in the interests of life after death. The rest of this letter precludes any such conclusion. Yet the contrast is between 'things above' and 'earthly things' (3:2). The reference to Christ 'seated at the right hand of God' is probably the clue. In harmony with the rest of his letter so far Paul is facing the readers with the challenge about where the centre of gravity for their lives is to be located. The false teachers offer a combination of secret knowledge about spiritual beings with rules and regulations about food, festivals, angel worship and self-abasement. By contrast Paul has repeatedly emphasized the Christian centre of gravity as our entering into Christ's death and resurrection. This is the clue to everything we do or say. To set one's mind on things above (3:2 –– see Philippians 4:8 'think about these things') is not to become other-worldly; it is precisely the opposite. It means to take all the affairs of life utterly seriously, as the rest of this letter will show, by seeing them all in the light of Christ's death and resurrection and our incorporation into them. We are to live every moment of life as those who are finished with evil in every form (dead to it) and committed to goodness in every form (risen to it). So 'seek' and 'set your minds' are a description of the intended course through life which the Christian sets for herself or himself.

Paul reinforces this position by a simple statement, which reads as a simple fact of life. 'For you died, and your life is now hidden with Christ in God.' That is how God sees it. That is how we see it. We may therefore test every part of our life, attitudes, intentions, words and deeds by this simple model— 'Is it hidden with Christ in God? Is it worthy to be described that way?'

Having said that Paul's teaching is not other-worldly, we must also notice that there is a contrast between here and hereafter. 'When Christ, who is your life, appears, then you also will appear with him in glory' (3:4). Present life is important; but it is not all-important. Because he died and rose triumphantly, we know that Jesus Christ is Lord of all. One day he will be seen to be so, and his faithful people will be with him. Midst all the pain and cost and hurt of standing for love, truth and justice in the world, we know that it will not always be like this. 'Glory' means 'the revealed presence of God'. The word 'appear' means 'the revealing of something previously hidden'. One day all will see clearly what now can only be perceived by faith. As we apply the gospel truth to life today, we are preparing ourselves for the glory to come.

If you go to an unveiling, you sit looking at the plaque, or painting, or sculpture covered over. Yet some in the room know what it looks like. The artist knows, so does the person who commissioned it; and so do the workers who covered it over! They are privileged ones who know what is to be revealed. So do we. How ought we to live, as those who know what life lies beyond the grave!

Prayer I'm grateful for today's reading as a balance to yesterday's. It almost seemed as though any principles for life might be suspect for the Christian. I now see the difference between guide-lines and rules. Thank you especially for the 'hidden with Christ in God' approach. I'll need time to work it out in every part of my life, but I'm willing to try. Please make me wise in the decisions involved.

Questions for consideration by individuals or groups

1. What dangerous teaching or habits do you think Christians today have to guard against, lest we be 'taken captive' (2:8)?

2. What do you take Paul to mean when he says that the fulness of God was present in Christ?

3. How, in the light of this week's studies, would you describe the meaning of Christ's death on the cross?

Put to death, therefore, whatever belongs to your earthly nature: sexual immorality, impurity, lust, evil desires and greed, which is idolatry. Because of these, the wrath of God is coming. You used to walk in these ways, in the life you once lived. But now you must rid yourselves of all such things as these: anger, rage, malice, slander and filthy language from your lips. Do not lie to each other, since you have taken off your old self with its practices and have put on the new self, which is being renewed in knowledge in the image of its Creator. Here there is no Greek or Jew, circumcised or uncircumcised, barbarian, Scythian, slave or free, but Christ is all, and is in all.

'Put to death therefore . . .'

Paul now gets down to details. Talking about dying with Christ and rising with him can be theologically interesting and liturgically meaningful (in our sacraments, for example). The question remains, 'What does it mean in daily life?' Paul now tells his readers. Verses 5–9 of chapter 3 contain the negative instructions, telling us what it means to die with Christ.

'Put to death' (3:5) is not a return to the imposition of ascetic acts like those Paul condemned in 2:16–19. He is now encouraging his readers to see how the dying and rising principle will apply in daily life. 'Sexual immorality' covers any sexual intercourse outside God's intended purpose of intercourse within marriage. 'Impurity' refers to any kind of moral uncleanness. 'Lust' is sometimes used of any kind of sexual perversion, but here it certainly means improper erotic passion. 'Evil desires' refers to any ways in which we enter into alliance with temptation instead of resisting it. 'Greed' can also be used in the sexual context, as it is for example in the Greek translation of Exodus 20:17, and as it seems to be in 1 Thessalonians 4:6. Or it may have a wider context of greed of any kind. Either way it is idolatry because it treats as a right that which is only a gift, and because it involves putting something else before God as the object of one's desires.

Two comments are important at this point. The first is that although this is an essentially practical section, and Paul is being embarrassingly frank, nevertheless he is operating very much at the level of attitudes and desires. The dying with Christ is no longer a theological theory or a liturgical act. It is reaching the deepest areas of human life, the source of passion and longing which issues in action. In this way Paul is dealing with cause not symptom, inward source not outward deed, and this is in sharp contrast with the false teachers at Colossae, with their rules for eating, drinking, festivals and angel-worship. It is also a sharp contrast with forms of Christianity today where either explicitly by rules or implicitly by what is known to be acceptable to

The farmers are busy in the fields,
Ploughing the land,
Scattering the corn,
To see what the land is going to yield —
Sown by the hand,
For new life to be born.

And this is a gift from our Father above,
Far up higher than the eagles can soar,
So let us scatter our own seeds of love,
To everyone, for evermore.

AMEN.

A Sunday School Scholar

the group, people live a certain kind of life through outward pressure, not inward compunction. It is the latter which produces true Christian holiness through dying and rising with Christ.

The second point flies in the face of much thinking about morals in our society today. It is simply that 'Because of these, the wrath of God is coming' (3:6). In a moral universe, playing fast and loose with truth produces its painful and destructive results. Moreover this is so because the God who created the moral universe is both moral and involved in the universe. In that sense every immoral act is an insult to him.

The readers used to be like that (3:7) but now evidently they are not. So other evil attitudes and actions should be put off, too. The word for 'rid' occurs often in the New Testament (Romans 13:12; Ephesians 4:22; 1 Peter 2:1). It reflects the need for determination to be done with evil. The idea of decisive action is also present in 2:11 and 2:15, describing Jesus' victory over sin and principalities and powers. It emphasizes the fact that even in our struggle against wrong attitudes and actions Christ has taken the initiative and our strength comes from being joined to him. The list in 3:8–9 is not exhaustive, but it provides adequate ground for us to prove Christ's presence with us.

John Sung was an oriental evangelist of enormous power and dramatic force. At one large meeting he wished to make the point about being rid of sin.

Seeing in front of him a row of flower boxes full of plants, he rooted one out to make a point. But all sins need uprooting, so he took up every plant in sight! It is not recorded whether he was ever invited there again, but the point about uprooting sins was not forgotten!

Prayer We're getting down to business now! I'm glad Paul doesn't stay in the realm of theory and theology only. The concentration largely on sexual sins must be related to the Colossian situation, but I remember Jesus's words about the attitudes being as praiseworthy or blameworthy as the acts. I note too that because Paul concentrates on sexual faults he is underlining the secrecy of many of our sins. Help me to take this challenge to my private world seriously, that you may be Lord there, too.

Lent 4/Monday   Colossians 3:5–11 (page 62)

'The new self'

The exhortation now takes a positive turn. Having told his readers what they are to be rid of, Paul now encourages them about the characteristics they are to develop. The language he uses is that of clothing. Having cast off unacceptable garments, they must now dress more worthily in terms of their Christian character.

He writes about the new self 'which is being renewed in knowledge in the image of its Creator' (3:10). The word 'renewed' literally means 'being made new'. This again emphasizes that the initiative and the work are God's. But the clue is knowledge. Paul comes back, again and again, to the importance of what we know in the Christian life. The place of the mind is crucial if we are to grow in grace. Any emphasis on experience or tradition or method will miss the point if it by-passes the mind. The basis of our growth as renewed selves is what we know God has already done for us in Christ, and what he wishes to do for us now. What he wishes to do for us now is spelled out in dramatic language. The words 'in the image of its Creator' bring immediately to mind Genesis 1:27, 'so God created man in his own image'. God is now evidently restoring what was lost through the ravages of human rebellion and sinfulness, as set out in Genesis chapter 3.

There is one significant difference, however. The word 'image' has already been used in this letter, at 1:15. There we saw Jesus as totally reflecting God's being within himself. God, in his present work in our lives, is not simply

64

restoring some original state of likeness to him. He is moving us forward to God-likeness which is related to the way in which he revealed himself in Jesus Christ. We have already noted the relevance of 2 Corinthians 3:18 to this process. We must now note it again. Growth in the Christian faith means growth in likeness to Jesus Christ, within our own lives. We are really back to the daily dying and rising with him.

The argument then takes an unusual turn. We would expect Paul now to list the qualities he looks for in such a life. Instead he gives the whole concept of the 'new self' a corporate interpretation. It is not only the Christian individual who enters into this transforming newness. The Christian community goes along this road too, and one of the signs that it is on the right track is its unity across powerful natural and social barriers.

Paul's list of such barriers is breathtaking when one considers the situation in the first century. 'Greek or Jew, circumcised or uncircumcised, barbarian, Scythian, slave or free' provides a list of insurmountable objects in the context of the day. Christians must overcome them all, according to Paul, as a sign of the new life in Christ (3:11).

It is, of course, appropriate to begin to understand Paul's comments in the life of the church itself. One of the saddest things about the history of Christianity is our failure adequately to abolish such barriers. Yet in many fellowships and worship services there is a great sense of oneness in spite of such divisions. It is one form of Christian testimony to the world.

Paul's point probably goes much deeper. It is that the ministry of Jesus is a condemnation of all ways in which one group of people adopts an attitude of superiority to any other group. Jews and Gentiles, masters to slaves, were two major examples in the first century. So was the attitude of men to women, to refer to Paul's similar list in Galatians 3:28. It is not meant to be true in the church only that such attitudes are removed. It should be true of the whole world. The church is to be a testimony and example of that.

This means that the people of God should be active in demolishing all forms of superior/inferior structures in our society, including white to black, rich to poor, manager to worker, employed to unemployed. The list can be considerably extended. Unless Christians are willing to demonstrate this practical application of the gospel to daily life we shall be denying a vision of God's love to many who need it.

Prayer I'm glad we're becoming more positive. It's exciting to think of the image of God being recreated within me. That really is an awesome thought. But I'm ready for it. The idea of all superior/inferior structures being demolished also draws out a deep longing from within me. Of course in both cases I see that I have a part to play too. Thank you for the examples in Scripture. Thank you for the image of Jesus Christ to guide me. Thank you that your power is now at work to make these things happen. I'm glad I'm part of it!

Lent 4/Tuesday   Colossians 3:12–13

Therefore, as God's chosen people, holy and dearly loved, clothe yourselves with compassion, kindness, humility, gentleness and patience. Bear with each other and forgive whatever grievances you may have against one another. Forgive as the Lord forgave you.

'Clothe yourselves'

We now read the list of the new 'garments of character' which will replace the disgraceful rags Paul told his people never to wear again.

Yet Paul still holds back the details as one further bit of theological understanding is given by the way he addresses them. The point of clothing themselves with the characteristics he is about to list is that they are 'God's chosen people, holy and dearly loved' (3:12). Each of these descriptions is applied to the Jews in the Old Testament. They knew themselves to be chosen, and went back through Moses to Abraham to demonstrate it. Their concept of holiness, of being set apart for God, kept strong their sense of belonging to him in the world. Prophets like Isaiah and Hosea reminded them how loved they were. Paul now gathers these great designations of Israel, the people of God through whom Jesus Christ came into the world, and applies them to the new Israel. They are chosen through Christ, holy through Christ, loved through Christ. Paul is asking what kind of behaviour would be worthy of people with that privilege. In 1986 I had the great honour of taking part in the Royal Wedding of His Royal Highness the Prince Andrew and Miss Sarah Ferguson. There was no question of wearing anything but one's best for the occasion. What kind of character should clothe those whose dignity is to be God's chosen people?

Now we come to the desired characteristics themselves. We notice again that they are not rules and regulations: they are attitudes to be adopted, from which the right deeds will flow (3:12–13).

The word 'compassion' can be translated 'ready sympathy' but it is actually stronger than that. One of the two Greek words used comes from the verb used by Jesus of the attitude of the Good Samaritan to the injured Jew whom he helped on the Jerusalem to Jericho road, help given against the tradition and feeling of centuries of enmity between Jews and Samaritans

(Luke 10:25–37). The word really means to be so deeply, inwardly moved that one must do something about the object of one's compassion.

Next is 'kindness', a generous spirit. One of the great characteristics of God himself is his generosity. The father of the Prodigal Son is an example of such a generous spirit (Luke 15:11–32). The despondent, guilty son returns with a speech admitting failure and asking to work only as a servant. He is met, incredibly, by the generous calling of a party to celebrate his safe return. Even his older brother could not bear that! But for such generosity to us, we would not be among God's people at all.

'Humility', or a humble disposition, comes next. There is nothing contrived about this. A great American scholar and preacher attended a ceremony in his honour. As he walked, in procession, onto the platform the audience began to applaud loudly. Without thinking he stopped, looked around and stepped back to make way for the important person receiving such a greeting. It only slowly dawned on him that he was the person!

'Gentleness' has been translated 'willingness to make concessions', meaning a person who is not always insisting on his or her own way. Of course it requires a certain inner strength and confidence not to feel threatened by needing to give some ground. Much unbending dogmatism springs from an inner lack of security.

'Patience' is also an attitude dependent on hidden qualities, particularly the ability to believe that God is in control, and that people have great inner resources to grow if helped. How patiently God himself prepared the way for the coming of Jesus Christ into the world!

'Bearing with each other' and 'forgiving one another' have their roots in the fact that we can only be what we are because God bears with and forgives us. We rightly get angry with the man in our Lord's story who was released from a debt of thousands of pounds but who then would not release a friend from a very small amount owed to him. We are angry, that is, till we see the point of the story!

Prayer Today's list of Christian qualities is rather like a collection of lovely flowers in a garden. They're all needed in order to give it a sense of wholeness and completeness. Each complements all the others. Weeds will only spoil the view! I'd like my life to be like such a garden, with only good qualities like kindness, compassion and humility flourishing more and more. Please do any weeding in my life that you deem to be necessary.

And over all these virtues put on love, which binds them all together in perfect unity.

'Over all these virtues put on love'

Although Paul's letter is written in the context of a struggle about true doctrine and right practice, his advice reaches a peak at a familiar point — the primacy of love as a Christian quality.

He made a similar point in writing to the Corinthians who were so proud of the many spiritual gifts they had (and they do appear to have been outstandingly endowed in this way). Having listed all the gifts, Paul argued that they belong together like the parts of a body, and that it is love which is the supreme gift (1 Corinthians 12–13).

It is similar argument here. The word translated 'binds' in Colossians 1:18 ('which binds them all together') literally means 'ligaments', to use one of our nouns as a verb. The inter-connecting feature in relation to all these desirable qualities is love. After all, love is the origin of all the others. Paul has addressed them as 'dearly loved' (3:12). Love is what motivates God's actions in Christ for our salvation (Romans 5:8, 'God demonstrates his own love for us in this: while we were still sinners, Christ died for us'). And love also gives some firmness to the other guide-lines. It prevents compassion from being sloppy, kindness from being mere indulgence of others, humility from becoming fawning, and so on. It gives them direction, too, because love seeks out those who need it most, and does what is best for them. A quiet reflection on 1 Corinthians 13, Paul's hymn about love, should be a regular devotional discipline for Christians.

The element of 'ligamenting' goes further than simply enriching all other qualities. It means that all the other qualities find a unity in love. It is significantly first in Paul's list of the fruit of the Spirit in Galatians 5:22, following a singular verb. It is almost as though all the other fruit listed there ('joy, peace, patience, kindness, goodness, faithfulness, gentleness and self-control') are extensions of love. It is love which holds them together.

It is important to distinguish between the gifts of the Spirit (as in 1 Corinthians 12 and Ephesians 4, for example) and the fruit of the Spirit (as in Galatians 5:22–23 and here in Colossians 3:14). The gifts are various in themselves, and are given variously to different Christians (Ephesians 4:11 — some to be apostles, some to be prophets . . .). No one Christian has all the gifts. They are spread across the Christian family in each place. By contrast all the fruit, the spiritual characteristics, are for all Christians. We may say,

'I cannot preach but I can administer'. We may not say, 'I cannot be patient but I can be humble'. But in both cases each gift needs all the others in the corporate life of the church, and each quality needs all the others in the individual life of the believer. And in both contexts it is love which gives the unifying power.

In the eighteenth-century Methodist revival a whole set of new ways of doing things was brought to life. Unlikely people discovered the gift of preaching, evangelizing, exercising pastoral skills, organizing local groups of Christians. There was a real risk that in such a setting the sheer volume and variety of new energies being released would be too much for any system to bear. What bound them all together in that turmoil was their affection for and loyalty to John Wesley himself. He was the unifying factor. In a much more profound way, midst the many gifts and fruit of the Spirit in the church today, it is God-given love and our love for him, which is the unifying factor.

We do well to think and reflect on the presence of spiritual gifts and qualities in our life, and ask that God will give us inner unity and corporate unity, through the love let loose on the earth in Jesus.

Prayer I pray for my local church today. Life there isn't always 'ligamented' together as it ought to be. I suppose that's because human beings see things differently, and because sin gets in, even where the life of the church is concerned. I ask that even when we disagree we may nevertheless love one another, and be bound together in the one body of Christ. Please let love give me an inner unity, too, so that I may be a model for the church in all I do.

Lent 4/Thursday   Colossians 3:15

Let the peace of Christ rule in your hearts, since as members of one body you were called to peace. And be thankful.

Let . . . peace . . . rule

With the best will in the world there can be friction and disagreement in a community of Christians, even between those who are seeking to act under the impulse of love. If we expect anything else then we become wrongly depressed, even disillusioned when it happens. In a group of fallible people, friction is always possible. In such circumstances, what are Christians to do?

Paul faces this issue by using an image from the field of athletics. The word translated 'rule' really means 'umpire'. Those keen on any kind of sport will know how important is the role of the umpire. Did the runners begin on the gun? Who crossed the line first? Was the foot in the right place? Did the batsman touch the ball now caught by the fielder? Was the forward off-side? These questions can only be answered in a way which allows the game to proceed if all the players accept the umpire's decision. Failure to do so threatens the teams, the current contest, and the sport itself. Players must abide by the word of the umpire.

It is for this reason that Paul, having been encouraging his readers to be active in rejecting unworthy qualities from their lives, and in putting on worthy qualities, now advises a much more passive role. 'Let the umpire's decision be final!'

But who or what is to act as umpire? The peace of Christ. This in itself is capable of various interpretations. Since the injunction is to let the peace of Christ 'rule in your hearts' it could mean that inner sense we have of being 'at peace' about something. If, day by day, we seek to be living under the guidance of the Holy Spirit, we know what this peace means. We also know its absence. We know what it is like not to be at peace, to feel uneasy, even deeply disturbed within ourselves, about some relationship, or action, or word, or thought, or future plan. Like a splinter in our skin, or a speck in one's eye, or a strain in a muscle, it makes us aware that things are not right. The peace of Christ acts as umpire here in that whenever we feel this disease, we search till we find its source, and we get ourselves into a healthy position again.

Yet we know that this, of itself, cannot be the sole guide. Our sense of being 'inwardly at ease' can be affected by other things too — like being under pressure, or illness, or tiredness. Our own inner sense cannot be the sole arbiter of the peace of Christ.

A second possibility is the corporate one. After all, Paul does write here in the plural 'in your hearts'. What is more, many of the qualities he has praised are about attitudes to and relationships with others. There is a corporate submission to Christ's peace as umpire. It is found as all the qualities adumbrated above are in operation; as people seek to work together, to understand one another, to be concerned for the well-being of others, to avoid dominating others, and so on. Behaviour which threatens the inner peace of the community may need to come under the stricture of the divine umpire. There is a corporate sense of the rightness or wrongness of something.

Yet even that alone may not be enough in practice, and does not exhaust the meaning of this verse in theological terms. In practice some Christian communities maintain a peace which steadily approaches the slumber of the dead! The peace is never threatened, because no one ever suggests anything new, disturbing or dynamic. That is not so much peace as somnolence. Theologically 'peace' has about it the deeper sense of a positive well-being based on knowing that God is in control, and on being obedient to his benevolent will. It is much, much more than the absence of war. It is the presence of a harmony with the divine purpose.

I don't believe we have to choose one of the three. It is in the inter-relation of an individual and corporate sense of peace, tested always by the concept of 'shalom', God's ordering of the world, that the peace of Christ acts as umpire.

Prayer This is a lovely picture of Christ's peace 'refereeing' the church. I focus my prayer first on any unease in my own life, asking for his peace to rule. I pray the same for my church, thinking particularly of people or situations needing this peace. Then I widen my vision and pray for the trouble spots of the world, asking that even where he isn't acknowledged his peace may somehow be sought and found. Give us your peace, O Lord!

Lent 4/Friday   Colossians 3:16–17

Let the word of Christ dwell in you richly as you teach and admonish one another with all wisdom, and as you sing psalms, hymns and spiritual songs with gratitude in your hearts to God. And whatever you do, whether in word or deed, do it all in the name of the Lord Jesus, giving thanks to God the Father through him.

'Do it all in the name of the Lord Jesus'

In looking at Paul's teaching on peace we noticed that beneath the individual and corporate sense of peace, there was the deeper issue of the meaning of Christ's peace, the grace-filled shalom of the Old Testament. As though to reinforce the importance of that third element, Paul moves on from the peace of Christ to the 'word of Christ' (3:16).

The word of Christ can mean either the teaching which Christ himself gave on earth, or the preaching about Christ which was the ground of their becoming his disciples. Again it seems unnecessary to choose. The teaching ministry of Christ is the only adequate basis for understanding what the good news about him should be. The gospel message as preached must always be tested for authenticity against the background of his earthly ministry.

Certain expectations about the word of Christ are important here. One is that the word translated 'dwell' means 'be at home'. Like many others, I travel a lot and stay in many different homes. It is a privilege to share in the homes of so many generous families. But in the end, there is actually only one place where I am truly 'at home' — in my own home, with my own wife and family. I know it intimately. It bears the marks of my living there. I am totally at ease and can be wholly myself there. None of it is shut off from me. Wherever I travel I still feel the excitement on returning. I'm coming home. Paul says that the word of Christ should be like that in our hearts — thoroughly at home.

Then there is the use of the word 'richly'. Our relationship to God's word is not meant to be a thin, poor, meagre affair. We are intended to be 'rich' in his word; that is, to be deeply conversant with it so that we are well-fed on it. From the new babes in Christ to whom Peter refers (1 Peter 2:2), craving for the milk of the word, we are to grow up into mature adults in the faith, knowing and understanding the word of God, and so obediently responsive to it, that it is at home in our lives.

Another point of great significance is the linking of the word of Christ to our fellowship with one another. Paul's use of the words 'as you teach and admonish one another' shows how the fellowship life of the church harmonizes with that of the preacher, since in 1:28 he used the same words, 'admonishing and teaching' of his work in leading everyone to maturity in Christ. The church which depends entirely on its preachers for growth, or which neglects formal teaching in the interests of fellowship groups for sharing, is each going to be on 'thin fare'. The formal preaching and the intimate fellowship need each other if we are to grow. In particular this is so because evidently the 'word of Christ' needs to be taught and applied personally in each new age and context.

We may be interested, too, in the link between 'the word of Christ' and the 'psalms, hymns and spiritual songs'. It is a word for us today. There is such variety in our worship, and so many different ways of worshipping God are being explored, and I support that whole-heartedly. At the base of all the changes, however, and at the root of much dissatisfaction with worship, is the fundamental question of meaning. What does it mean to worship God, and how may we discover meaning in it as we do so? Unless we address these questions, no amount of variety will achieve the fulfilment we seek. And the question of meaning is addressed by the answer in the 'word of Christ'.

From the detail Paul now steps back once more. Everything is to be done 'in the name of the Lord Jesus' (3:17). Life is not divided into religious and secular: it is all for Jesus, and we should be able to know him everywhere. Only so can we honestly give God thanks in everything through him.

Prayer It isn't easy to picture the church congregation teaching and admonishing one another. Some might not like to do it, and even more might not like to receive it! But I can see how naturally it follows from loving you, and loving one another for your sake. Help me to see how our church could begin to move down that path, and how I can play my part. Maybe our worship of you would begin to have more meaning then.

Lent 4/Saturday   Colossians 3:18–19

Wives, submit to your husbands, as is fitting in the Lord.

Husbands, love your wives and do not be harsh with them.

'Wives, submit . . . Husbands, love'

If the teaching of the word of Christ is to be done, and if admonition is to be given, then Paul must himself get down to more practical detail. He does so by choosing controversial areas of human relationship; that is, areas of life which the advent of Christianity made controversial. Christianity laid the foundation for freedom in areas with which even now we still struggle.

This is particularly so with the relationship between husbands and wives. What follows is written in the context of 3:11, and the abolition of group superiority or inferiority. Paul does not deal with who is inferior or superior, but how each finds his or her role in God's purposes.

There is also another context, the first-century Roman world. In that setting few would have doubted the absolute authority of husband over wife, father over child, master over slave. Instructions to wives to submit to husbands would cause no stir at all. The parts of Paul's teaching more likely to surprise first-century readers would be the assertion in 3:11 that all are one in Christ, and then the demands he made upon the husbands, fathers and masters. These were the new elements which laid the foundation for freedom in each of the relationships outlined.

We must, therefore underline the fact that when the question of rights and responsibilities is raised it is the rights of the wife, child, slave that are new, not the other way round. As one commentator puts it, 'the claims of the slave are as real as the claims of the master'.

Most important of all, the predominant theme throughout this section is neither husbands, fathers, masters on the one hand, nor wives, children, slaves on the other. The paramount claim to be established is that of the Lord himself. In verses 10–25, the Lord is mentioned six times. The stress is not on individual rights and responsibilities within themselves; it is how each relates to all the others in the light of the relationship of each to the Lord. This is a sharp reinforcement of the approach of 3:11.

My own belief is that Paul begins with the accepted social relationships of his time. He lifts them into the context of the gospel, which immediately shifts the focus from person-to-person dominance, to one of submission of all persons to the Lord. He then, in this context, establishes rights for those considered inferior — wives, children, slaves — in a way which points to their liberation. Yet he does not raise a battle cry in these matters, lest the gospel came to be renowned for the wrong reasons.

In verse 18–19, on husbands and wives, Paul tells wives to do what they were expected to do any way! The idea of their having a choice in the matter is a gospel insight. He tells the husbands to love their wives, and that in the setting of serving the Lord is an unexpected demand. The relationship of each to the other is in the context of 'in the Lord'.

I end this section with two, perhaps delicate, observations. In communities and churches where there is a strong formal emphasis on women being submissive to men, there is often in their private lives a high incidence of dominant women. On the other side, modern whole-hearted liberation movements often end up ignoring unhelpfully the general differences in configuration between the male and the female in a way which causes confusion initially and chaos ultimately. By contrast Paul's teaching places first-century relationships into the context of God's love for Christ in a way which both acknowledges differences between men and women, and allows for the steady influence of divine love which enables each to be enriched within the relationship. One pattern is not enforced forever.

Prayer We really are into delicate territory now, Lord! Paul has traditionally been blamed for being somehow 'against' women. I see now that it was the men he was really getting at. Even clearer is the predominance of all our relationships being 'in the Lord'. In that setting no one should treat anyone else as less than a full human being, whatever their formal relationship. For today I ask that all my dealings with those nearest to me will be informed by love and truly 'in the Lord'.

Questions for consideration by individuals or groups

1. What insights into being a Christian have you gained from these passages?

2. What place have peace and love in the Christian life? Is there anything we could do to make them more central?

3. What conclusions do you draw about your husband/wife relationship on a basis of Paul's words on that subject to the Colossians?

4. What difference should it make to our lives to 'do it all in the name of the Lord Jesus'?

— A PRAYER —

Lord, I've tried to pray, but find it hard to know what to say.
I hope I'm better at writing to you.
It is a beautiful day here; was it like that on Palm Sunday? Not that it matters, Lord, rain or shine, it was Jesus' triumphant entry into Jerusalem that mattered, not the weather.

Lord, can you help me? Why is the road of life so much harder for some than others?

Lord, why are we not at peace with ourselves?

Lord, why do we make promises and then break them?

Lord, why don't we praise you more?

Lord, I realize I have asked a lot of questions, and since I began I think you have spoken to me.

I can hear you say, 'Be like Jesus, ride calmly down the road as he did on Palm Sunday. Put all your trust in me as Jesus did, and I will not fail you.'

Lord, I feel better already — I will try harder, and perhaps, just perhaps, I may make it to the end of the road and you, one day.

AMEN.

An adult church member

Children, obey your parents in everything, for this pleases the Lord.

Fathers, do not embitter your children, or they will become discouraged.

Slaves, obey your earthly masters in everything; and do it, not only when their eye is on you and to win their favour, but with sincerity of heart and reverence for the Lord.

'This pleases the Lord'

The principles laid down for husbands and wives are now applied to the parent and master relationships. The strongly authoritarian context of the first century must be borne in mind, and also the contempt for the lives of the masses which was often reflected in the attitudes and actions of the leaders and nobility.

The obedience of children to parents (3:20) is carried over from the Jewish heritage of Christianity, but it is firmly planted in the new context — 'for this pleases the Lord' (3:20). The parent is no longer the absolute object of authority or submission: children are to look through their obedience to parents and see the Lord as the one whom they serve.

In the same way, but much more unusually, the fathers are to reflect the attitude of the Lord when their children are called upon to obey. 'Do not embitter your children, or they will become discouraged' (3:21) could almost be read as a commentary on God's dealings with the people of Israel in the Old Testament. Hosea 11:1–11 is a most moving account of God's way of being father to his people, loving and winning them back in spite of their waywardness. The model of divine fatherhood is the pattern for the human Christian father in that setting.

The beauty of this way of construing relationships is that on the one side there is a set of clear guide-lines, yet on the other there is room for adaptation in each new context. The way a modern child expresses obedience to his father will bear little resemblance to that of the first-century child. The same should be true of the way a modern father expects such obedience. The important thing is that this is a component in the relationship and that, for both of them, the relationship is exercised 'in the Lord'.

The same is true, and this must have been much harder, for the master/ slave relationship. The sting of subservience to an earthly owner is drawn by the injunction to obey 'with reverence for the Lord'. This enables it to be offered 'with sincerity of heart' (3:22). Whether being watched or not, whether they will gain anything by it or not, they will work hard for the Lord.

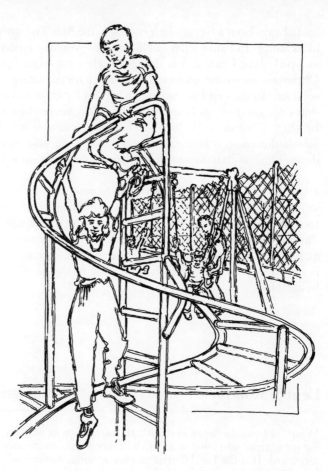

The history of the Christian church carries many examples of how this works out. My home area is the north-east of England, where Methodism flourished in mining communities. Perhaps the major reason for growth was the obvious and dramatic change that took place in the lives of those who were converted, some of whom had previously lived dissolute lives. It showed at work, too, and one result was that Methodists became trustworthy. Their fellow workers trusted them, with money and with negotiations on their behalf. The management trusted them as reliable men who would keep their word. This is the origin of the strong link between Methodism and the Trade Unions in the mining areas. They did it as for the Lord.

That it could not end there, in the situation of masters and slaves, is obviously clearer to us than it was to the first-century Christians, for whom it had always been a fact of life. Yet even in the New Testament there are signs of a change. In Paul's letter to Philemon the vexed question of the case of the escaped slave Onesimus is discussed. He escaped to Paul, and is now a Christian, but in law belongs to Philemon, a friend of Paul's. There is no ideal solution. In the end Paul believes it is right for Philemon to have Onesimus 'back for good — no longer as a slave, but better than a slave, as a dear brother' (Philemon 15–16). Much of the future dissolution of slavery is foreshadowed in that simple sentence; yet even now much remains to be done. The foundations were laid: we are extremely slow to build on them.

Prayer What a long time history takes to make, Lord! Even now we struggle with parent/child relationships, and with management/labour relationships, too. We took ages to get rid of slavery even though Paul's teaching undermined it centuries ago. How slow we are to allow the 'in the Lord' attitude to be expressed in our relationships as actions. Wherever I am involved with others, I ask that 'pleasing to the Lord' may determine my behaviour.

Lent 5/Monday   Colossians 3:23–4:1

Whatever you do, work at it with all your heart, as working for the Lord, not for men, since you know that you will receive an inheritance from the Lord as a reward. It is the Lord Christ you are serving. Anyone who does wrong will be repaid for his wrong, and there is no favouritism.

Masters, provide your slaves with what is right and fair, because you know that you also have a Master in heaven.

'As working for the Lord'

This section seems to continue to address the slaves, since we do not get the advice to the masters until 4:1. Yet the near-repeat of 3:17 shows that this way of looking at things applies to all.

Paul develops a little further the idea of working for God. There are two separate elements in the teaching here. One is a clear statement that masters, 'bosses', are never as important as they think they are! In the first century the masters actually owned their slave workers. The slave had virtually nothing that was his own except his life. The demand of the master was seen as absolute, total. Paul's teaching shows that not to be the case. The only unconditional demand on our lives is made by God, and he alone has the right to make it. Every other demand is relative to the one demand of God, and that demand is made in love, as the whole of this letter shows. What Paul is here enjoining upon his readers who are slaves is therefore a view which in attitude already sets them free. They were forced to serve their earthly master. Paul offers the option of choosing to serve their heavenly Father, using the earthly master as an avenue along which this service is offered. Far from reinforcing slavery, therefore, Paul was loosening its hold considerably. Once slaves cease to 'think slave' they are well on their way to being free. As the book *Roots* showed, one of the hardest tasks in setting slaves free was to enable them to conceive it, want it, and believe it could happen. Paul started that process in his letter to Colossae.

This harmonizes very significantly with the teaching of Jesus. Luke records some statements of Jesus in Luke 14:25–35, which are often viewed as some of the hardest things Jesus ever said. In fact they are amongst the kindest. His teaching simply exhorts his hearers to budget everything for God. Put everything into the one budget, meeting the absolute demand of God on your life, and everything else will be seen to be relative to that one demand. That is the secret of true freedom — budget everything for God. I once visited a woman who had heard me expound that passage. During the night her pregnancy had to be terminated, and she lost her baby. I was deeply distressed for her, and visited her, trying to offer some consolation. She looked me straight in the eyes and said, 'Don't worry, please. I had budgetted for the possibility.' The listener had understood the implication of the talk better than the speaker.

The other implication of Paul's advice here is that what happens in this life is not the most important thing, unless its atmosphere and outlook are the same as the atmosphere and outlook of heaven (3:24). The consolation of working for the Lord, however hard that work is, is that we are already in the atmosphere of heaven. That is the real 'inheritance', the real 'reward' (3:24). It is not 'pie in the sky when you die'. It is to recognize and live now by the deeper things in life than earthly possessions and status. This is why the voice of the Lord is today so often heard from the communities of the poor and underprivileged in the world. At the World Methodist Council at Nairobi in 1986 the most significant presence, in my judgement, was that of the group of South African Methodists, some of whom had been imprisoned for their Christian witness. They showed evidence of a depth of Christian perception, and a breadth of Christian freedom, which most of the rest of us lacked.

The masters should not miss this point, either. They too have to answer to the Master who truly rules all. The thing we should pray for above all else for world leaders is a sense of awe in the knowledge that they too are answerable to the only one who can make unqualified demand on human life. In the end the door of exit is the same shape for all. The masters are also servants.

Prayer I have a feeling Paul's advice to the slaves applies much wider. Certainly this distinction between that one ultimate demand on my life and all the other relative demands is pretty basic stuff — and very demanding, too. Help me to take it with absolute seriousness, Lord. I'll do an audit of my life, with your help, to be sure every part of it is, as far as I can tell, under your control. I can see that I'm only really free when everything is safely in your hands.

Lent 5/Tuesday   Colossians 4:2–4

Devote yourselves to prayer, being watchful and thankful. And pray for us, too, that God may open a door for our message, so that we may proclaim the mystery of Christ, for which I am in chains. Pray that I may proclaim it clearly, as I should.

'Pray that God may open a door'

This letter is now moving towards a close. Shortly there will be greetings to a whole variety of people. For the moment, however, there are some personal comments.

First there is the reminder of the importance of prayer. In some ways it is the most significant part of the Christian life in that it is both the most hidden element and the one that most depends for its meaning on the existence of God. Paul has told his readers how much he prays for them and what he prays for them. If we are finding our prayers becoming somewhat dull and stilted we could benefit by studying the prayers in the New Testament and modelling our own on them.

The word Paul uses about prayer life ('Devote yourselves to prayer') comes from the liturgical side of his vocabulary, and has about it a strong note of perseverance. In days when there is a high premium on 'excitement' and 'happenings' in connection with spiritual activity, we do well to remember that the main reason for praying is not how we feel but that it is a true and necessary thing to do. In prayer we offer ourselves again to God; seek to be aware of his will for the world and for our lives; devote ourselves afresh to that purpose; lift to him the needs of others and our own needs; and reflect on the world in his presence. These things are vitally necessary to our discipleship, whether we get excitement in them or not. We need to persevere in them because of their intrinsic value in fulfilling the kingdom of God.

Alongside prayer Paul puts watchfulness and thoughtfulness. The former links up with his warning from the outset (2:8). It is also reminiscent of the words of Jesus in the Garden of Gethsemane, to disciples who were drowsy with tiredness and fear (Mark 14:38). Under the pressure of false teaching, with a struggle going on, Paul's readers need to watch carefully. Jesus also used these words to warn his hearers to be ready for the end of all things, when the struggle may become more difficult (Luke 21:34–36). There is an example from the past and a warning for the future. Between these two, watchfulness should accompany prayer.

So should thankfulness. Seven times in this letter Paul has encouraged or expressed thankfulness. It seems to be the punctuation sign for everything else. As one mature Christian put it, 'The only trouble with counting my blessings is that when I do it I can never get right through to the end of the list.' Thankfulness to God is an antidote to diseases of the soul and assaults of the devil. I have a friend who makes great use of birthdays and anniversaries, his own and others, as focal points of thanksgiving and prayer. Thankfulness is not that part of prayer that we must go through out of good manners, when we really want to concentrate on requests! Pause to be truly thankful, and the requests will take on new meaning altogether.

At last Paul asks them to pray for him (4:3–4). Characteristically, it is not for his own well-being — it is that he will have opportunity, and skill, in preaching. There is a lovely humorous irony about his request that God will 'open a door for our message . . . for which I am in chains'. The messengers may be imprisoned, but the message can get out, as Paul claims in Philippians 1:13 that it had done. It may be that the main reason for our failure to evangelize is not the lack of opportunity but the absence of intention.

Prayer I've been saying some new prayers this Lent, Lord! Now I thank you that even these prayers have kept me in the tradition going right back to Jesus himself. I daren't put my prayers with those of Jesus in Gethsemane, but I thank you that I can try to pray at the entrance to that garden, even though the disciples found that so hard to do. I'm not under their pressure, but please let me be watchful all the same — and thankful for all your great goodness to me. Oh, and I ask you to bless all evangelists today, as they seek to make your word known.

Be wise in the way you act towards outsiders; make the most of every opportunity. Let your conversation be always full of grace, seasoned with salt, so that you may know how to answer everyone.

'Make the most of every opportunity'

Although Paul inveighs against the allegedly secret knowledge of the false teachers at Colossae, he does acknowledge that there is a difference between insiders and outsiders, between those who are committed to Christ and those who are not. He asks his readers to be wise in the way they behave in relation to outsiders. One or two points are worth picking up here.

First, Paul did intend the Christians to have dealings with non-Christians. His emphasis on Christian growth and discipleship is not meant to be at the expense of outside contacts. One fears that churches can take up so much of their members' time that they have none left for the evangelistic witness they are exhorted to make! It takes courage to break the mould. I heard a pastor in Australia describe how he had deliberately set aside one night a week to go to a leisure centre for sporting recreation. To his own great surprise, there had been a steady stream of conversions amongst the customers, and most recently the manager himself had become a Christian!

The encouragement to 'make the most of every opportunity' (4:5) can cause us some tension and make us least likely to be of use. The language used however may help us. The word rendered 'opportunity' really means 'time'. It is the word to describe a particular moment of time, as opposed to the steady passing of time. And it is often used in the New Testament to mean a significant moment in time, when God acts in a special way to make it a moment whose importance is out of all proportion to its length. These are 'God's moments'. One commentator called them moments of truth and destiny. Then the word translated 'make the most' really means 'to buy up', with the sense of concentrated activity. It is probably meant to conjure up the picture of the market tradesman buying up a whole range of goods, 'cornering the market'. The point which emerges from this may well be that God is at work turning ordinary moments into moments of truth and destiny. It is his work, his mission. Yet we are invited to use all our skill and commitment to share in his work as we try to 'buy up' every moment usefully in his service. We are neither sole operators nor initiators. We are junior partners in God's business.

Their conversation is to be 'full of grace, seasoned with salt'. The word 'grace' reminds us again that our aim is to be channels of God's grace. We belong to the body of Christ only because of God's grace. We may now be those through whom that grace will reach others. A study by an American denomination showed that eighty per cent of people joining the church did so because of the influence upon their lives of family members, neighbours, friends or working colleagues. It was not primarily the preaching which initially attracted, but the lives of others. 'Seasoned with salt' reminds us that in the first-century Middle East climate only salted food did not go bad.

Henry Martyn was an outstanding missionary in the last century. He gave his life to overseas work, never being able to marry the lady he loved so dearly. In the end he was driven to death by the remorselessness of a driver taking him on a journey. You might think that these are the ingredients for a grim, melancholy life. Yet it was said of Henry Martyn that he was the life and soul of every party he attended.

'So that you may know how to answer everyone' (4:6). It is assumed that our lives create the question which our words can then answer. How sad to have an answer if our lives don't provoke the question. Equally how sad to provoke the question but never give the answer!

Prayer Yesterday I prayed for evangelists to be able to preach the gospel with power. Now today I find I'm put on the spot. How many non-Christians do I know well, I ask myself? Do they know I'm a Christian? And have I ever prayed for the opportunity to tell them, and taken that opportunity when it came? Maybe I need to get to know more non-Christians anyway. As I do, please let my conversation be like the salt that enriches and preserves. And please stay close to me, because I'm nervous about this bit of the journey!

Lent 5/Thursday   Colossians 4:7–9

Tychicus will tell you all the news about me. He is a dear brother, a faithful minister and fellow-servant in the Lord. I am sending him to you for the express purpose that you may know about our circumstances and that he may encourage your hearts. He is coming with Onesimus, our faithful and dear brother, who is one of you. They will tell you everything that is happening here.

'That you may know about our circumstances'

This little section provides us with a view of some of Paul's team, many of whom we know little about yet who were crucial to the spread of the gospel.

At the heart of it all is Paul's human desire for his readers to know how he was getting along, and for their hearts to be uplifted. This gives a slightly different perspective on the apostle who seems so often to be austere, serious and perhaps too busy for personal considerations. How wrong we can be!

Tychicus was a native of Asia. He accompanied Paul to Jerusalem (Acts 20:4) probably taking the money that had been collected. In 2 Timothy 4:12 he is sent by Paul to Ephesus. In Titus 3:12 he is likely to be sent to Titus. He is another of those eminently trustworthy people on whom God's Kingdom is built. How carefully churches need to produce and cultivate such men and women. To Paul he is a dear brother, a faithful minister and a fellow servant. You could not wish for a better testimonial than that.

The combination of Paul's circumstances and their encouragement is an interesting one. Paul was, after all, in prison, probably never to leave it again. The great travelling preacher is locked up in chains. Yet somehow those who come to bring this information are meant to 'encourage the hearts' of the Colossians.

The point is an important one. The Christian's joy and happiness is not intended to depend on his or her circumstances. This is one great distinguishing feature about those who follow Christ. His own ministry was one of privation, loneliness, misunderstanding, betrayal and finally persecution. Members of his own family did not understand or support him. The religious leaders to whom he appealed resented and opposed him. Even his own followers understood only dimly, and at his moment of greatest need, largely deserted him. The Roman Governor intended to be generous but gave in to Jewish pressure. Yet it is this teacher whose Beatitudes in the Sermon on the Mount are about being happy, whose life changed and healed so many others, who walked in total peace all through his ministry, whose love conquered even death. Out of the worst event of all God brought the best news of all. The secret is not good circumstances, but the loving life of God which gives peace and joy and grace to triumph over untoward circumstances.

Paul's advice to the Philippians is 'Rejoice in the Lord always' (Philippians 4:4). He also rejoices in the Lord at his readers' renewed concern about him (Philippians 4:10), but a little latter claims that he has 'learned to be content whatever the circumstances' (Philippians 4:11). How can you persecute people like that? F. B. Meyer used to tell of a lady he had met who suffered many personal tragedies yet retained a serene and ever-deepening faith throughout. When Meyer, the great preacher, asked how she had survived all these events, she told him that when she received a parcel she didn't spend her time admiring the packing and the string. She opened the parcel to see what the gift was. So it was, she claimed, with everything that happened to her. Within the circumstances she looked to perceive the presence and goodness of God.

Onesimus is another 'faithful and dear brother'. He may well be the former slave from the letter to Philemon. His name means 'useful'.

Prayer Lord, I confess how easy it is to let my circumstances determine my mood. Happiness is so closely related to 'things going well'. I suppose there's really nothing wrong with that so long as I don't lose my joy when things go wrong. Thank you for people who are an encouragement and comfort to me. Help me to give such loving service to others. I'd also like to be like those reliable Christians I've been reading about. And please make me 'Onesimus' — useful.

Lent 5/Friday   Colossians 4:10–15, 17

My fellow-prisoner Aristarchus sends you his greetings, as does Mark, the cousin of Barnabas. (You have received instructions about him; if he comes to you, welcome him.) Jesus, who is called Justus, also sends greetings. These are the only Jews among my fellow-workers for the kingdom of God, and they have proved a comfort to me. Epaphras, who is one of you and a servant of Christ Jesus, sends greetings. He is always wrestling in prayer for you, that you may stand firm in all the will of God, mature and fully assured. I vouch for him that he is working hard for you and for those at Laodicea and Hierapolis. Our dear friend Luke, the doctor, and Demas send greetings. Give my greetings to the brothers at Laodicea, and to Nympha and the church in her house. . .

Tell Archippus: 'See to it that you complete the work you have received in the Lord.'

'Give my greetings'

It was usual to end with greetings, our letters often do. But these letters provide insight into the human resources of the gospel at that particular time. They also encourage us to see that the earliest Christians were also human, as we are, and equally fallible. The list of Paul's fellow workers should make us feel quite at home.

Aristarchus was on the journey mentioned in Acts 20 (see verse 4). He was one of those seized by the angry silversmiths at Ephesus when Paul only just escaped. Two years later, as Luke records in Acts 27:2, he was travelling with Paul to Rome. Now he is a fellow prisoner. 'A good faithful friend in all circumstances' seems to describe Aristarchus well.

Mark's name conjures up an entirely different scenario. Mark was there in Acts 12:25 and 13:5, but 13:13 tells the sad news that John Mark left Paul and his companions and returned to Jerusalem. In 15:37 when Paul and Barnabas were planning a new missionary journey, Barnabas ('son of encouragement') wished to take Mark; Paul did not. On the strength of that disagreement they made two separate journeys, Barnabas taking Mark, Paul taking Silas (15:39–40). Paul's reference to instructions about Mark arouses the curiosity! But the Colossians are to welcome him if he comes. In 2 Timothy 4:11 Paul says that Mark could help him if he can come. In Philemon 24 he is a 'fellow worker' of Paul.

Mark should be an encouragement to us all. He could not always meet the demands made upon him, but he did, in the end, become a good servant of the Lord. We must frankly wonder, however, what would have happened to him if Barnabas had not taken such a generous, forgiving line with him. Paul does seem to have got it wrong at that point — another encouragement to the rest of us!

Jesus, called Justus, I know nothing about. Epaphras we have looked at already. What a prayerful, earnest, devout and industrious young man he was. Paul tells the 'folks back home' that they can be proud of this one of their own. Luke the doctor seems to be the one whose account in Acts traces the story of the growth and spread of the early church, and shows when he accompanied Paul and when he did not.

Demas requires his own paragraph. At the time of writing he is working well with Paul, evidently. But 2 Timothy 4:10 says sadly, 'Demas, because he loved this world, has deserted me and has gone to Thessalonica'. Again Paul shows little sympathy for a deserter. Again too (2 Timothy 4:11), Luke is mentioned. We could only guess at why Demas had gone. Even a fellow missioner with Paul was not thereby automatically preserved in full faith and discipleship. 'Let him who thinks he stands be careful lest he fall.'

Greetings go to Laodicean brothers who are to read this letter too and to Nympha and the church, her house. The house church movement has a long tradition!

Archippus evidently needed a stern word about completing the task he had started (4:17). The word describing his work can be translated 'diaconate'. We do not know what it was, though it might be the collection of money for the Jerusalem church. Archippus is probably the person of that name mentioned in Philemon 2. Some think he was Philemon's son.

What a mixture they were, just like us! We also have in common the grace of God enabling weak, fallible but gifted human beings to do his will in the world. We may like, in the atmosphere of this section of the letter, to reflect prayerfully on our immediate brothers and sisters in the faith.

Prayer Lord, I'm rather relieved to read about Christians in the first century who didn't always get it right. Even the great Paul seems to have been wrong about Mark. And poor Mark had a bumpy start on his journey of Christian leadership. So maybe there is still room for me! I'm grateful for Barnabas, too. Help me please, to be an encourager of others. Let Demas be a warning to me, and let me, like Archippus, finish what I begin.

Lent 5/Saturday   Colossians 4:16

After this letter has been read to you, see that it is also read in the church of the Laodiceans and that you in turn read the letter from Laodicea.

'This letter . . . the letter from Laodicea'

Paul gives a particular double instruction at this point in the closing greetings. They are to read this letter then see that the Laodiceans get it too. (Why only they are selected we do not know.) Then the letter to Laodicea is to be read at Colossae. Was that the letter we know as the letter to the Ephesians?

This raises the wider question of how the early church retained any sense of belonging to a unity. As the church spread, and new communities sprang up in many places, there could be the link with the first evangelist, as in Paul's connections with the church at Corinth, for example (1 Corinthians 2:1–5). Then there were workers who travelled about and would keep Paul informed, as Epaphras evidently did in the case of Colossae (1:7–8), as did Tychicus (4:7–8), Onesimus and Timothy (4:9–10). Then there were traders who travelled and brought news, like Chloe and her household (1 Corinthians 1:11). And there were the gatherings of Christian leaders, as at Jerusalem (Acts 15).

In all these comings and goings, there was clearly much preaching, teaching and sharing. The pattern set out in Acts 2:42 probably indicates the general content, though references elsewhere to hymns, psalms and spiritual songs (as here in Colossians 3:16), and to the ministry of the gifts of the Spirit (as in 1 Corinthians 14) suggest a fuller picture, and a varied one. In each case, however, there was the presence of preaching and teaching. The tradition was maintained in this preached form, as Paul seems to suggest in 1 Corinthians 15:1–8, and especially verse 3, 'what I received I passed on to you as of first importance'.

There must also have been training given in connection with baptism and the Lord's Supper. Passages like Romans 6:1–23 outline the meaning of baptism. In 1 Corinthians 11:17–34 there is an example of the understanding of the Lord's Supper on which the practice was based.

Apart from these various, and somewhat haphazard, links, much depended on the letters, and particularly those of Paul, if there was to be any continuity and comparability of teaching and understanding. The pattern of these letters is therefore instructive about how the content of the gospel was construed.

After the traditional greeting, usually Christianized both by reference to the Father of our Lord Jesus Christ and to the combination of 'grace and peace', Paul often rehearsed how he had any link with the readers, and then told of the frequency and content of his prayers for them. In other words the initial setting is an affirmation of God's grace, and a reflection on human experience of it.

There then usually follows a doctrinal section, often linked to whatever the situation was in the church or churches addressed. In Romans he sets out the gospel message to show he was a true apostle who understood what it was about, possibly as a preliminary to visiting them. In Corinthians it relates to the many disorders there. For Galatians it is to safeguard them against going back into Judaism, Here in Colossae it was to combat an incipient form of gnostic heresy. Each is addressed by the gospel message, rehearsing particularly those parts of the message which were especially relevant.

Next there comes the practical implications of such doctrine, usually introduced by 'then', 'therefore', 'wherefore' or 'so'. In this part he explains how people ought to live who believed that kind of doctrine.

He ends with greetings.

The letters sustained and safeguarded the early church. We are wise to note their shape as well as their content, and to order our lives accordingly.

Prayer I can imagine how exciting and important an event the arrival of a letter from Paul must have been in the first century AD. I give thanks for the growth and stability of the early church, in spite of the haphazard way it was serviced. How rich we are in opportunity, by contrast with them! Let my appreciation show in my attendance at the means of grace. And may this pattern of doctrinal belief determine my behaviour and become deeply engrained in my Christian life.

Questions for consideration by individuals or groups

1. What does Paul mean by 'making the most of every opportunity'?

2. What do you make of Paul's fellow workers? Have we anything to learn from them today?

3. How did the early church grow in understanding and size?

Palm Sunday   Colossians 4:18

I, Paul, write this greeting in my own hand. Remember my chains. Grace be with you.

'I, Paul, write this greeting'

The letter ends, as it began, with Paul's name, but there is a difference. The letter has probably been written by someone else at Paul's dictation. Now the apostle signs his own name and writes this very last section.

This is not the only letter where Paul puts something in his own hand. In 1 Corinthians 16:21 and in Galatians 6:11 the same thing occurs. It is not altogether clear why it happens in these but not in others. It could be that there is some reason for special affection here, though in that case one might have expected Philippians to be the candidate, since that is the happiest of his letters. It might be that the three letters with some handwriting of Paul's are those in which there are strong words about false teaching and false behaviour. The personal note would be a way of assuring the readers that his vehemence is against false teaching and teachers, not against the general readers.

It may, alternatively, be that Paul is wary of counterfeit letters alleged to come from him as in 2 Thessalonians 2:2 and 3:17. If that is the true reason, then it is yet another reminder that the early church grew in days every bit as difficult as ours.

'Remember my chains' (4:18), may be a reminder of the circumstances in which he now finds himself, and a plea for sympathetic prayer as a result. Commentators generally find that less than convincing as coming from Paul. It is hardly typical of his approach. Most favour the idea that it is a sign of his apostolic authority. He is in chains, following the Master who called him, and who warned him of what he must suffer for his sake (Acts 9:16). If the

Colossians need apostolic authority for his teaching, they will find it in the fulfilment of their Lord's own word to Paul at the beginning.

'Grace be with you' makes a normal final greeting, and a benediction. But it also sums up the letter. The foundation of their faith was laid in the grace of God, through Jesus Christ whose total ministry reflected the fulness of God made man. By God's grace they have responded to that ministry, through people like Epaphras, one of their own. By grace they have not only believed in the death and resurrection of Christ, they have been gathered into it, as their baptism signified. They are counted by God, in Christ, to be dead to sin and alive to new life. By grace they must now live in the strength of that dying and rising every day; discarding all the shabby clothing of sinful attitudes and actions, and being clothed with the Christian characteristics which show Christ-likeness. By grace these will be worked out in all their relationships.

Today we enter Holy Week. We could hardly have a better greeting, on Palm Sunday, to launch us on that journey, than 'Grace be with you'. We will seek to understand some of the great themes of Colossians, in relation to the experiences of Jesus on his way to death and resurrection. If we can enter sympathetically into our Lord's last days, grace becomes almost tangible. We discover the depth of the faith in such a way that, as Paul told the Colossians, we shall not need to turn elsewhere for spiritual sustenance and meaning. We have everything in Christ.

Prayer I'm sorry to be ending this letter, Lord. I feel I've got to know Paul, and his friends, rather well. Thank you for their company on this journey of discovery. They didn't grow easily, did they? 'Grace be with you' just about sums up why they survived at all. They certainly needed it! And so do I. May I know that grace more deeply because of this letter from Paul, and may I have everything in Christ. As Paul would wish, I end on a note of sincere thanks for all your goodness to me.

HOLY WEEK REFLECTIONS

Monday

Battle for the truth

Our study has not yet faced the rather obvious question, 'Why did Paul bother to write to a church he had never visited?' No doubt it was an issue for some, at least, of the Colossian Christians. They had their own leaders and their own structures. Why would this comparative outsider interfere?

Part of the answer, of course, lay in Paul's friendship with Epaphras, one of their own young men. No doubt there had already been considerable links along that line. And there were others with Paul who appear to have been known by Paul's readers, if the final greetings are to be taken at their face value. Yet none of these, of itself, was enough to justify a letter of this kind.

The reason was, to put it bluntly, that the truth was being threatened and someone had to do something about it. False doctrine was being taught, doctrine which, in particular, belittled Jesus Christ by locating the experience of salvation elsewhere than in his death and resurrection. There was also an emphasis on outward activities as necessary to salvation, whereas the Christian faith is primarily about the building of inner Christian character which then expresses itself in appropriate conduct, but which allows for the relating of inner qualities to different contexts. In short, some Colossian Christians were in danger of being imprisoned in erroneous belief and practice. Paul could not sit back, even in prison, and simply allow that to happen.

This week, in the church year, we particularly remember how our Lord did the same thing, though on a massive scale. His disciples knew what the result of coming to Jerusalem would be. Thomas, as usual, spelled it out with crystal clarity — 'Let us also go to Jerusalem, and die with him there' (John 11:16). By coming to the heart of things Jesus was putting himself into the hands of those who most wanted him out of the way. He was coming to the place where they were at strength, and at a time when crowds could be incited. Conflict was inevitable.

The reason Jesus constantly gave for making this journey, recorded by Mark's gospel with monotonous regularity (Mark 8:31, 9:31, 10:33) was simply that, 'The Son of Man must go to Jerusalem and suffer . . .' A further comment in Mark 10:45 is simply that 'For even the Son of Man did not come

PALM SUNDAY HYMN

Chorus
So come and praise the Lord our God,
Praise to David's Son.
He came to save us from our sins,
The victory He has won.
God bless the King of Kings,
He comes for you and me,
Telling us of his good news,
He meant us to be free.

1. He came riding on a colt
   Amidst the cheers and waves.
   He came to tell the world about
   The lives that He can save —

   Chorus

2. The crowd did not expect to see
   This peaceful, humble King,
   But when men really understand
   The world will follow Him.

   Chorus

3. So let us praise the living God
   Like those of long ago,
   And live the life He planned for us
   And so our faith will grow.

   Chorus

Two teenage girls; they also wrote music to
accompany these words

to be served but to serve, and to give his life, a ransom for many'. For the salvation of the world, such confrontation and cost were necessary.

To the Colossians, as we have seen, Paul wrote of 'filling up what was lacking in the sufferings of Christ for his body, the church'. There is a continuing of the confrontation for the sake of the spread of the gospel.

How are we to respond to this in Holy Week?

We must note first that the major struggle for truth in the world concerns evangelism, telling out the good news. If people do not hear they cannot respond. Yet this is not an easy task. There has to be the commitment by God's people, especially at local church level, and the allocating of resources. We need reflection on how to reach people, and on what to say when the opportunity arises. And we need first to share our story with one another.

But there is social caring, too. So many people are in need in our world society. To struggle for the truth includes doing all we can to show the love of God in our actions. This will also require a certain lowering of our standard of living in order that others may benefit.

There is also the struggle for justice. How can we serve a God of love who gave a world for all to enjoy, if we do nothing about unjust structures in our society? It is doubtful if peace will ever come without justice.

Jesus went to Jerusalem at enormous cost because the salvation of the world required it. For him it was the way of truth and obedience. Paul followed his footsteps in his battle for the gospel to prevail. As we follow this week, what will we do?

Prayer Teach me, O Lord, so to love the truth of your word that I will defend it from falsification and misuse. May I also put the truth into practice as I share its meaning with others, serve those around me in need, and struggle for justice in our society. Let me not bear lightly the wrongs which others suffer, but rather give my life that all may have the chance to enjoy your kingdom on earth. I ask this for your name's sake. AMEN.

Tuesday

'Each belongs to all the others'

One of the unexpected insights one gets in reading the New Testament letters concerns the other people with whom leaders like Paul, worked. In Colossians, for example, Timothy and Epaphras are mentioned early on, then a whole host of others figure in the greetings. Some seem to be trustworthy in all circumstances. One needs a special commendation. One is reminded of his responsibility. One who at present is involved will eventually leave that work altogether.

These people are given precious space in a limited letter, not just because their work is valuable and the readers need to know where they are, but also because spiritually and naturally Paul needs them. From time to time even this stalwart servant of Christ, who can boast to the Philippians that he can be content in any situation, nevertheless writes 'no one is with me' or 'send this one, or that one'. His links with God were unbreakably strong. He never doubted his Lord's provision for him. But he needed people, too; and rightly so. Members of his team, however much they depended on him for leadership, ministered to him by their friendship and presence. When he was in prison they kept in touch with the outside world. How else could the Colossians receive their letter?

In Holy Week we reflect on our Lord's need for his disciples, too; and on how variously they were able to respond to his needs.

He needed them to understand what his ministry was seeking to achieve. At times they had magnificent surges of inspiration, 'You are the Christ, the Son of the living God,' replied Peter to the question of Jesus about his identity (Matthew 16:16). Yet in seconds he is being rebuked severely for attempting to prevent Jesus going to Jerusalem (Matthew 16:23). For the most part the disciples followed 'at a distance' in their understanding. Wanting to believe, and willing to be used, they could nevertheless just as easily end up arguing over who would have the chief seats in the Kingdom of God! On the Mount of Transfiguration Peter's enthusiasm for building commemorative tents showed how little he had grasped what was going on (Matthew 17:4–5). James and John, the other two disciples present, said nothing, but this is no indication that they understood what was going on any more than Peter did.

At Gethsemane Jesus needed companionship, in prayer and sensitive presence, as he fought the crucial spiritual battle involved in going on to Jerusalem and to death. Three times he emerged to find them drowsy with sleep (Mark 14:32–42). When he was arrested they all ran off (Mark 14:50). Peter and John followed at a distance, with disastrous results in Peter's case (Mark 14:66–72). It was the women who were faithful right to the end (Mark 15:40–41).

In our devotional reflections during this special week we may focus on particular points. For example, we are often despondent because we and other Christians are not as good, perceptive or effective as we should be. Even our Lord himself had to put up with very second-class material. (Paul, writing to the Corinthians, makes a point about how low down in the world's estimate the Christians at Corinth would come, which he uses to demonstrate that it must be God's power which has established the church! — 1 Corinthians 1:26–2:4.) Inadequate though they were, and would continue to be, Jesus left the work to them, and by God's grace through the Holy Spirit, they were greatly effective.

We need also to ponder the fact that Jesus needs his disciples at least as much today as he did then. This is why Paul develops the picture of the church as the body of Christ, its members the instruments of his work in the world, using together the many gifts he has given to them (1 Corinthians 12).

This leads naturally to point number three. We need each other. To be accepted by Christ is to be accepted into his family. Paul's words in Romans 12:5 are worth further quiet reflection — 'So in Christ we who are many form one body, and each member belongs to all the others'.

Prayer I thank you, Father, for the human ties within your family, the church. Help me to cherish and love those you have given to me as brothers and sisters in Christ. Forgive me that, like the earliest disciples, I too easily misunderstand, lose heart, and fail you. May I, like them in such moments, discover again your gracious forgiveness and restoration. Let me learn from failures and grow by successes so that my life may be pleasing to you. I ask this prayer through Jesus Christ your Son. AMEN.

Wednesday

'Watch and pray'

In his letter to Colossae Paul puts 'watchfulness' and 'prayerfulness' together as necessities for a healthy Christian experience. It is a significant piece of advice, not least because it picks up the use of these words together in the ministry of Jesus.

For Paul the watching involved in the Colossian setting was probably related to the false teaching circulating there. In this context they are to watch out for error, to hold to the truth *embodied* in the life, death and resurrection of Jesus; *contained* in the gospel, the 'word of truth' (1:15); *experienced* in their dying and rising with Christ, so powerfully symbolized in baptism; and *applied* in their daily lives and relationships. The events, the tradition and the experience belong together.

These links and relationships do not automatically continue to be right and true, however. For that, watchfulness is required. People develop preference for certain parts of the ministry of Jesus Christ, and take exception to others. The tradition contained in the message comes under pressure from cultures and ages through which it passes. The power of human experience is also great, causing the message to be altered to fit the particular thoughts and feelings of individuals and groups. The church must watch if it is not to go astray.

Significantly, Paul does not give this advice only to the leaders of the church. It is the task of the whole community. Preachers and teachers are answerable to God for their work, not only directly and ultimately, but also through the congregations and classes. They are not required simply to sit, listen, obey and do all that we advise. They are to listen, test, sift and share in the common watchfulness of the whole people of God. A preacher who gets no 'come-back' from his or her congregations is in a very exposed situation.

For Jesus the watchfulness related to the pressing events of Gethsemane and all that followed (Mark 14:38), and to the last days before the end of everything. Watchfulness in those contexts still related to truth, but had much more to do with perceiving the meaning of developments around one, and clarity about what to do at the time which would be true and faithful. Sadly, in the Garden of Gethsemane, his chosen disciples were able to do neither.

The references to prayer have slightly different connotations for Paul and Jesus, too, because of the different contexts. Paul tells his readers what his prayers are for them — a mixture of thankfulness and anticipation of their growth in understanding, character and strength. He also asks their prayers for his evangelistic ministry. For Jesus the situation is much more desperate. The enemy is at hand. The disciples are to be left alone. The crucial battle with the forces of evil is about to take place. Salvation for the world is involved in the unfolding story ahead. His prayer will be, and theirs should have been, for courage and strength to go through that battle against the forces of evil in the universe.

We may feel our setting is more like that of Paul and the Colossians than Jesus and the disciples. And we will be right. Yet our involvement in the gospel through our allegiance to Christ means that we are also part of the unrelenting battle against evil and for good in the world. Watchfulness to preserve true faith and true discipleship; and prayerfulness for perception of what is happening around us, and courage to live faithfully, are as necessary now as ever. In Holy Week we commit ourselves anew to this path.

Prayer Grant me, Lord, the patience to watch, and the grace to pray; that between watching and praying I may discern your path for my life and your strength for my service. Let me be wise to avoid temptation; if it comes, strong to resist temptation; and at all times courageous in thinking, saying and doing what I believe to be right. So may I be sensitive to your will, obedient to your purposes and useful in the world, for Jesus Christ's sake. AMEN.

'Wisdom in relating to outsiders'

In writing to the Colossians Paul gave remarkably little time to the question of those outside the church. His concentration is on the internal difficulties of doctrine and practice faced by the believers. Of course much of what he wrote would affect outsiders, in the sense that more effective Christian living is a better witness. But at one point he specifically mentioned outsiders, telling Christians to be wise in using their time meaningfully, and in having conversation which, like salt, brings life and combats decay. He then completed his sentence with the explanation 'so that you may know how to answer everyone' (Colossians 4:6).

The implication is clearly that Christians ought to expect to have conversations of some substance, about the faith, with non-Christians. Paul also encourages his readers to believe that they will be able to give satisfactory answers to questions raised by those who are not disciples of Jesus.

There are two implications in what Paul wrote. One is properly to hear the question. The other is to have an adequate answer to give.

Paul is himself a good example of how to do both. If we study Luke's account in Acts of Paul's visit to Mars Hill in Athens (Acts 17:16–34) we will find a model for this way of proceeding. Left alone in Athens, Paul studies the city, then has opportunity to debate in the Areopagus, with a group of people who, Luke says, 'spent their time doing nothing but talking about and listening to the latest ideas'. He began his speech with reference to their city and an inscription there (17:22–23). Knowing that his audience contained both Stoics and Epicureans, he continued with an affirmation of things which he and they have in common (17:24–28). Then he begins to draw the reins in somewhat. God has overlooked ignorance, but now calls for repentance (17:30). It is all the more urgent because a day of judgement has been fixed. The proof of this is the raising from the dead of the man through whom the world will be judged (17:31). He had begun where they were, selected from his understanding of the gospel message those things which best fitted their attitude, and slowly introduced these till he can call for repentance in the light of God's work in Jesus. He proceeded from there to Corinth where, as he told the Corinthians later, his message was very different (1 Corinthians 2:2), because Corinth was different from Athens.

We may note the sensitivity of Jesus to those around him, too. He went to people where they were, and spoke to them about things and in language which they understood. His conversation with the Samaritan woman at the well, recorded in John 4:1–42, is a classic illustration of this. She was a Samaritan woman, and not a very moral one by all accounts. Yet he was not reluctant to speak to her, a man to a woman, a Jew to a Samaritan, a rabbi to an immoral person; and he talked about fetching water! By the end, however, he had led her to faith. We have much to learn of that art.

The other implication of Paul's reference to outsiders is that we should be willing and able to deal with objections and questions. The task of understanding major criticisms and answering them, is called apologetics. We need to help one another to handle such situations. The church as a whole needs more commitment to this task also, producing scholars who hear the objections and provide thoughtful, convincing responses. If we fail in this task, much of our evangelistic activity will encounter very solid resistance. The seed will simply fall on hard ground.

However humble and slight we feel our faith to be, we can try to begin where others are and take the opportunities given to explain why we believe. And we can pray for those who fulfil the large intellectual task of defending the faith.

Prayer I pray, O God, for those who carry the heavy task of defending the faith in our modern world. Make them sensitive in discerning true objections, wise in providing responses, and convincing in declaring their faith in Jesus Christ. And help me, God, to be able to give a reason for my hope in the gospel to all who will listen. I ask this that your kingdom might come and your name be glorified, through Jesus Christ our Lord. AMEN.

Good Friday

Dying with Christ

No matter how one approaches it, Good Friday is bound to be a sombre day. With the most open attitude possible it is difficult to avoid a feeling of injustice about the events of that day, and of deep sorrow that such an evidently good person should end his life in this way. I manage to feel sorry, too, for those caught up in the system of prosecution involved. Pilate, the Roman Governor, was in an impossible situation. He did not really understand what the fuss was all about, but he was under enormous pressure from Jewish leaders for this rabbi to be put out of the way. Those leaders themselves were also involved more deeply than they probably understood. How does one fulfil one's responsibility to protect the faith, particularly when a young upstart teacher is making such dangerous claims for himself and such severe criticism of those in authority? The law was clear.

It is as though they were all caught up together on a journey whose destination was already determined, and yet a journey also dependent on the free decisions each of them was making. The disciples did not have to run away. The Jewish authorities could have found other ways. Pilate could have acted differently. In other situations he had provided strong opposition to Jewish wishes. Even the crowd did not have to join in as it did. All these participants in the journey played their part. They all bear responsibility.

Yet the greatest responsibility lies on the shoulders of the one who, as far as everyone else was concerned, had least to contribute. He was, after all, the prisoner, being taken from place to place under guard, with little say in the matter. Or had he? If he had stayed away from Jerusalem it would never have happened, as his disciples told him. He need not have waited on the Mount of Olives for the soldiers to come and take him prisoner. He could have ensured a much better interview with the High Priest and he could have helped Pilate to let him off. For some reason he could not, or would not, or both.

On the way to Jerusalem he kept saying that the Son of Man *must* go to Jerusalem, with all the consequences that would follow. Further back still there was the meaning of his baptism, and his words about the bridegroom being taken away after the wedding feast. There were references to the baptism with which he must be baptised, and the cup he must drink. He told his followers that they must learn to carry a cross. He said the Son of Man would lay down his life as the ransom price for many. When all this is read in the light of Old Testament prophecies like those of Isaiah 53, one begins to understand that this figure at the centre of it all, apparently under the power of the authorities, was in reality the prime mover in the action. He did what he must do, and what he chose to do. That is the meaning of his prayers in Gethsemane.

How are we to respond to all this on Good Friday? First we must ask why he did it. Peter's answer on the Day of Pentecost, as Luke records it in Acts 2:36, is that God in raising him from the dead, has declared him to be both Lord and Christ. The only proper response is to repent and be baptised, so that 'in the name of Jesus Christ your sins may be forgiven' (Acts 2:38). Christ's death has broken sin's stranglehold on humanity. The supreme act of perfect love has loosed the grip. We need no longer be under sin's control, as Paul teaches so clearly in Romans 6:1–18.

There is one wonderful central insight from the Protestant Reformation of the sixteenth century. It is that God in Christ has done for us what we cannot do for ourselves — set us free from the power of sin. We can thank God for that today. How we respond to it is food for tomorrow's reflections.

Prayer I thank you, O Lord, for this sad and joyful day. Sad because a perfect man died unjustly. Joyful because we know that in dying he dealt sin a death blow, in being tied to the cross he set us free, in breathing his last he made life available to us all. Help me today to enter into that mystery, like him to seek and do your perfect will at whatever cost, and so be truly a disciple. In Jesus's name I pray. AMEN.

Easter Eve

'Buried with him'

The message of the Cross, as we thought about it yesterday, can produce at least two immediate responses. One is the sense of gratitude that God's love should be so freely and fully expressed. The other, sometimes following later, is unease lest it somehow is not right for someone else to do such a thing for me, and doubt whether it can make much difference anyway. On the Eve of Easter we need to take such doubts head on.

We can begin by admitting that there is a way of presenting that message, and a way of responding to it, which justifies such feelings of unease. If the death and resurrection of Jesus are presented as happening in history, with the meaning that God will forgive those who believe, and if it is accepted simply with mental assent or emotional disturbance, or both; then we do have grounds for questioning. Mental and emotional acceptance of events in history leaves much to be desired. It becomes what one scholar described as 'the manipulation of theological counters', like some form of ecclesiastical chess. And it can leave our lives largely unchanged, except for allegiance to church and its activities. Any doctrine of substitutionary atonement understood like that is probably immoral and blasphemous.

It is not the whole biblical view, however. There can be little doubt that the Bible teaches that Jesus bore in our place what we could not bear ourselves — the consequences of our sins (Mark 10:45; Romans 3:21–26; 2 Corinthians 5:14, 21; 1 Peter 2:24).

It is equally clear, however, that what is expected of us in response is much more than believing it happened, or even believing that we are forgiven because of it, or even being grateful that it is so. We are called to be 'gathered

Extract from a report of an Easter Worship Workshop

'One of the great attractions to me of the art workshop is that the only requirement for anyone to attend is the willingness to participate. As no specific skills are required, it is open to all to join in and try their hand at one or more of the art disciplines as they wish. And as always in a venture of this kind, there is the surprise at discovering the latent talent within the members of the congregation — most often a surprise to those members themselves. The workship provides the setting for a valid working expression of faith, utilizing the varied media of the arts. Some can express their faith by the use of their hands, some by their voices, depending on their own talent or interest. It provides the setting for a real exchange of ideas, feelings and beliefs, perhaps only possible outside the more formal framework of the church service, and for an extension of community spirit. These ideas came together finally in a service of worship on Easter Day which to me offered a diverse but unified expression of faith and a fresh sense of commitment to the Christian message. Through the media of art, music, drama, poetry and collage, we had expressed a new understanding of the age-old truths, and I believe this communicated itself to the members of the congregation that day who had not come along to the workshop evenings.'

A teacher who led the drama workshop

into' his death and resurrection so that, in one sense, they do become ours.

This is what Paul means in the verse from 2 Corinthians 5 which we quoted earlier. In verse 14 Paul writes, 'We are convinced that one died for all, and therefore all died'. What Jesus did was so truly done on our behalf that it really is as though we had done it — 'one died for all'. The conclusion must be that those who know this to be the case must live accordingly — 'therefore all died'. What will be the outcome of that? It will be that 'those who live should no longer live for themselves, but for him who died for them and was raised again' (2 Corinthians 5:15). We could not, of ourselves, have struggled victoriously against all the powers of evil in the world. Only God's Son could do that. And he did it for us. What we can do, however, is to follow him down that road, and be counted as dead to sin and alive to God in Christ in dying to all that is unworthy and rising to all that is good and lovely and true.

I explained this point at a Conference. Some days later I received a letter from a friend. She said she had gone back from the Conference and attended church on the Sunday morning. There another woman, with a rather 'sharp tongue' had been critical and hurtful. She always managed to get under my friend's guard. Feeling hurt, my friend went home, knelt at her bed and consciously 'died with Christ' to the angry, resentful feelings she had towards the other woman. Quite wonderfully she felt a new spirit of forgiveness enter her life. It really did not matter that such things had been said. She could still love and forgive. Her letter ended by saying that she hoped I would go on telling people these things — so I am now telling you!

Prayer For this quiet space I thank you.
Father, as I remember Good Friday, and prepare for Easter Day, may I remember the meaning of this time for Jesus too. On this day he lay buried, awaiting resurrection with power. Help me, Lord, to know what it is to die with Christ to all that put him to death, that I may also have the resurrection to new life. So may this great day be for me a time of deeply spiritual renewal. I ask it for His sake. AMEN.

Questions for consideration by individuals or groups

1. How can we guard the truth of Christianity today?

2. Discuss the unity of the Christian church in the light of our reflections this week.

3. How do you understand the idea of 'dying and rising with Christ' and what difference does it make to the experience of the Christian?

'Risen with him'

One of my greatest privileges, as a minister of the gospel, is to open worship on Easter Day with the words 'Christ is risen!' It is even better if the congregation know to respond with 'He is risen indeed!' The privilege is even greater if, as minister, you have travelled with your congregation through Lent, Holy Week and Good Friday and if a bare church is now transformed into one bathed with flowers. You see the meaning of the day written on the faces of the congregation, too.

Resurrection Day operates at a variety of levels. There is something about 'feeling' resurrection. I learned from Bishop Lesslie Newbigin the story of Bukharin, one of the Russian Communist leaders, going to Kiev early in the revolution, and giving a one-hour address to a large crowd on the value of atheism. At the end he invited comment or question. A young Orthodox priest got to his feet and shouted 'Jesus Christ is risen!', to which the crowd replied with a loud 'He is risen indeed!' There was no logic to it, but they knew (felt) it to be right.

There is a philosophical, theological level to it, too. Resurrection is about meaning for life. At least it addresses the question of what life is about. There is the theological question about *what it means* to say that Jesus Christ was raised from the dead. But there is the even deeper issue of what it says to life as a whole — namely that divine love cannot be destroyed from outside by any other force. It is stronger — in its vulnerability — than the forces of evil, apathy, human selfishness and callousness. It has power to cure our pessimism in face of the evidence around us, and to redeem our cynicism about human nature. Above all, it means that we can look forward with hope. I recall being very deeply moved when a leading Christian layman in the context of a group of us sharing our Christian story with one another, said that to him the resurrection made all the difference between meaning and meaninglessness in life. Without it, there seems to be little point; but with it . . .

A third level concerns what I might call our inner understanding of Christianity itself. It says something, for example, about who Jesus was and is. Paul affirms, in Romans 1:4, that he 'was declared with power to be the Son of God by his resurrection from the dead: Jesus Christ our Lord'. In his ministry there had been many actions, much talk and breathtaking claims. The test was what would happen when the combination of the authority of rulers and the sentence of death did their work. For a while his disciples felt all to be totally lost. On resurrection day, however, he was wholly vindicated. Neither sin nor death could hold him.

It also has meaning for us. As we have constantly noticed, we do not simply 'know about' his resurrection, nor simply 'believe' it: we are 'gathered into it' — we are risen with him to new life in Christ.

Lastly, literally, it says something about our attitude to death. Because he has risen for us, we too have a confidence in life beyond the grave. We dare to believe in that life, though we cannot see it, just as surely as we believe there is land beyond the horizon though we cannot see that either. As John Wesley used to say, 'The best of all is, God is with us', and 'The best is yet to be'. We have everything in Christ.

Prayer Thank you, God, for this happiest day of all. Our Lord is risen from the dead, and we with him. Let all that I am praise my risen Lord, and join him in the risen life of those who gladly serve him. May the worship of all your people sound out across the world in a paean of praise, for love has triumphed over sin and death, and we are free.